SCHAUM'S *Easy* OUTLINES

HTML

BASED ON SCHAUM'S
Outline of HTML
BY DAVE MERCER

ABRIDGEMENT EDITOR
CHRISTINE SHANNON, Ph.D.

SCHAUM'S OUTLINE SERIES

McGRAW-HILL

New York   Chicago   San Francisco   Lisbon   London   Madrid
Mexico City   Milan   New Delhi   San Juan
Seoul   Singapore   Sydney   Toronto

DAVE MERCER is President of AFC Computer Services, a Web site and database design company. He has been designing data bases since 1993 and Web sites since 1995, using a variety of languages, including Paradox Application Language, PERL, HTML, VBA, VBScript, and SQL. He is from Spring Valley, California.

CHRISTINE SHANNON is chair of the Computer Science Program and Margaret V. Haggin Professor of Science at Centre College in Danville, Kentucky. She previously taught at Georgetown College in Kentucky and was a visiting professor at the University of Kentucky and Cornell University. She received a B.S. degree from Marygrove College in Detroit and both her M.S. and Ph.D. degrees in mathematics from Purdue University, and an M.S. in Computer Science from the University of Kentucky. She is the author or co-author of several professional articles and papers.

1 2 3 4 5 6 7 8 9 AGM AGM 0 9 8 7 6 5 4 3 2

ISBN 0-07-142242-0

Contents

Chapter 1
INTRODUCTION TO HTML

IN THIS CHAPTER:

- ✔ Origins of HyperText Markup Language (HTML)
- ✔ The HTML Specification
- ✔ The Structure and Function of HTML
- ✔ Browsers and Servers
- ✔ How HTTP Works
- ✔ The Document Object Model (DOM)
- ✔ Other Web Page Languages and Scripting
- ✔ Web Page Design

Origins of HyperText Markup Language (HTML)

HTML was created by Tim Berners-Lee in collaboration with Robert Caillau while they worked at CERN in 1989 (CERN is a high-energy physics research institute in Geneva). It is a subset of Standard Generalized Markup Language (SGML). The pur-

1

pose of SGML is to provide a common convention for creating languages for communicating information in documents. People creating documents with SGML languages *markup* their documents by inserting commands (called *tags* in HTML). These tags define the appearance and workings of the document when it is viewed in an appropriate manner.

The goal for HTML was to create a platform-independent language for constructing hypertext documents to communicate multimedia information easily over the Internet. Using an Internet protocol called HyperText Transport Protocol (HTTP), HTML documents could be transmitted to any user on the Internet and displayed by software called a browser.

The HTML Specification

There is an organization called the World Wide Web Consortium (W3C). It is the responsibility of this organization to maintain and update the formal specification for the HTML language.

Rather than continuing to develop HTML, the W3C has begun recasting HTML into XHTML, a more formal version of HTML that follows the design principles of extensible Markup Language (XML). XHTML is covered in Chapter 9, and XML is covered in Chapter 10.

 Useful information!

You can get the latest information on HTML at the W3C Website located at www.w3c.org.

The Structure and Function of HTML

The following code shows a minimal HTML document that can be displayed in Internet Explorer or Netscape Navigator:

```
<HTML>
<HEAD>
<TITLE>The Title</TITLE>
</HEAD>
</HMTL>
```

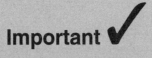

Important ✔

Most HTML tags have both a beginning and ending (or closing) tag. The beginning tag is enclosed in angle brackets (<>). For example, the first tag you will ordinarily see in an HTML document is <HTML>. At the end of an HTML document, you will see the ending HTML tag (</HTML>).

Browsers and Servers

When you open your browser and connect to a Website, your browser sends a request to the Web server software of the Website you wish to view. The request contains a surprising amount of information about your location on the Internet, the type of browser you are running, and what you are requesting. The Web server software on the other end interprets the request, and if everything is in order, it sends you a copy of the appropriate Web page. Your browser, in turn, interprets the Web page received by reading the HTML tags and then displays the result on your screen. The format or protocol used for communicating these requests and responses between browser and server is called HyperText Transfer Protocol (HTTP).

How HTTP Works

As the name suggests, HTTP is a protocol used for transferring hypertext documents across the Web. A *protocol* is a specification for communicating information

URLs

URL stands for Uniform Resource Locator. The word *Uniform* in this case means that the syntax follows a standard convention, even when extended into new addresses. *Resource* means anything that has an identity, such as a file, a program, an image, and so forth. A URL includes the following components:

- http://—The http refers to the overall *protocol* being used, and following that must be the colon and two forward slashes.
- The name of the *host computer* on which the resource resides. Typically this is the domain name (for example, www.e4free. com).
- The *port* on which the Web server is listening—this is typically 80, and must be preceded by a colon (:). This is usually omitted and assumed to be :80. Ports are logical addresses to which messages may be sent in an operating system.
- The *absolute path*, preceded by a forward slash (/), to the folder where the file is located, including the filename. For example, a typical URL might be www.e4free.com/asubfolder/afile.htm.
- If there is a *query* attached to the URL, it begins with a question mark, and the name/value pairs in the query are separated by ampersands.

Note!

Often you can omit the filename because the Web server has been programmed to automatically look for the filename index.html.

Requests and Responses

In a request from a browser to a Web server, the first line is called the Request Line. The Request Line includes the Method, the URL, and what version of HTTP is being used. Methods include the commonly used "GET" and "POST", among others. The "GET" method is designed to retrieve whatever output is associated with the request, and the "POST" method is designed to insert the contents of submitted forms.

In a response from a server to a browser, the first line is called the Status Line. The Status Line includes the protocol version and a numerical status indicator code followed by a short reason phrase. For example, 404 Not Found is a common status code and reason.

The Document Object Model (DOM)

HTML 4.01 is associated with a Document Object Model (DOM). An object model is a representation of the relationships of various functions, objects, collections, properties, methods, and so forth within a particular language, technology, or application. The purpose of the model is to allow people to review and analyze those relationships, so that they may more easily understand how to work with them.

The DOM for HTML is considered an application-programming interface (API) for HTML documents (and XML documents as well). It uses traditional object-oriented programming techniques to define the objects that make up an HTML document. The DOM allows developers to build documents in which the objects contained in them can be navigated and modified in real time. For example, the BODY element has an attribute for background color. In the DOM, the BODY element can be thought of as an object with a collection of attributes. These attribute values can be altered, changing the existing background color from one to another, in response to events affecting the BODY element. JavaScript is capable of reading and changing background colors in a Web page.

Other Web Page Languages and Scripting

One of the most common languages included in Web pages is JavaScript. It finds its way into so many Web pages because most browsers can process JavaScript commands without special help.

You Need to Know

JavaScript is called a scripting language because it doesn't need to be compiled. Instead, it is interpreted at run-time within the browser. It runs slower than a compiled program, but since Java scripts are usually very short, the difference in speed is usually not noticeable.

To insert functions created with JavaScript in a Web page, the SCRIPT element is used, as shown here with a simple JavaScript:

```
<script language = "JavaScript">
function pushbutton() {
            alert("Hello!");
}
</script>
```

The function defined can then be called from within the body of the page using a variety of methods based on object events, as in the following example using the OnClick event of a FORM element (a button named Button1):

```
<form>
<p><input type="button" name="Button1"
value="Press Here" onclick="pushbutton()"></p>
</form>
```

Practical Extraction and Reporting Language (Perl) is another common scripting language. An extremely simple Perl script is shown in the following example:

```
#!/usr/local/bin/perl
#prints Hello World back to the user
print 'Hello world.';
```

Programmed Hypertext Preprocessor (Php) is a server-side scripting language that can perform functions ranging from simply feeding data back to the user to full database search, retrieval, and data processing. Here is a simple example showing common Php syntax:

```
<?php echo "Hello World<p>"; ?>
```

You might also see Microsoft's Active Server Pages (ASP) scripts such as the following one that feeds back a statement to the user:

```
<%Response.Write "Hello, world" %>
```

Web Page Design

One of the first considerations when creating a Website must be the type of functions it is required to perform. For example, some Websites are meant to convey large amounts of technical information, while other Websites are mainly for entertainment.

To determine the functions a Website should perform, it is important to establish objectives. Objectives help to focus the Website to one or more specific tasks, such as sales, customer assistance, the distribution of information, and so forth. As the user performs these tasks or processes with the assistance of the Website, the results can be measured. Measuring results helps you determine whether or not the objectives of the Website are being met.

Once objectives are established and functions are defined, it is easier to proceed to the physical design of the Website. Ease of use—usability—is always an important factor in Website design, but usability must often be balanced with capability and flexibility.

Bandwidth is also an important consideration in the development of Web pages and Websites. As a general rule, the size of Web page files should be kept to a minimum, to make downloads faster and cheaper for users, and to reduce the Website owner's transmission costs.

Usability and Page Layout

Usability engineering and marketing go hand-in-hand when designing the page layout and structure of a Website. Usability engineering is the practice of testing the usability of a particular product or service, and in the context of Website design refers to examining the user interface (the part of the Website seen by users in their browser) for ease of use.

Important idea! ✔

Combine usability data with marketing data to form a page layout and Website design that is easy to use and at the same time communicates well.

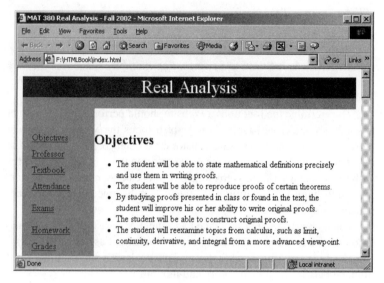

Figure 1-1

Figure 1-1 shows a typical Web page design. Across the top there is a banner, down the left-hand side there is a menu of links or buttons, and in the larger right-hand side of the page the content of each page appears. This layout is well-known and easy to use.

Platform or Browser Dependence

HTML is said to be platform-independent, but the look, feel, and workings of a Website still depend rather heavily on the browser software used.

Each browser understands common HTML tags, but usually not competitors' tags. In addition, newer versions of a browser may recognize more recent tags than older versions, even within the same brand of browser.

Note!

Designers should use only the common denominator HTML tags or code several versions of a Website so all major browsers and versions are covered.

One of the details passed by the browser to the server during a request for a page is the type of browser. By checking the browser type, your Website can automatically send back Web pages appropriate for the browser type and version.

Storyboarding the Website

The primary focus of Website design with HTML is the front end, or user interface. These are the pages and functions people see directly on their screens. Since a Website can be thought of as a series of screens people see, a storyboard can be used to rough out the content, look and feel, and navigation of each page. Usually a Website storyboard will also include lines showing the links connecting each page.

The storyboard can be done using plain paper and pencil, rapidly drawing and discarding ideas while the client offers input. A good technique for arriving at a useful design is to start with the premise that no idea is bad and simply draw and include them all. Then, begin to weed out features that are unnecessary in terms of the objectives. The result will be a storyboard that allows developers to make pages that are easy to understand and navigate and that fulfill the client's objectives.

Website Content Development

Content is the word used to describe all information communicated within a Website, meaning text, graphics, programmed functions, video, audio, 3D, multimedia, and so forth. Content development can be as simple as entering text into a page or as complex as a complete video production formatted for delivery from a Website. Deciding what content to include in a Website depends upon the objectives of the Website and the tastes of the designer and client.

Text content can be gathered from existing hard copy material or written from scratch.

Graphics can be produced from digital photographs, scans of hard copy photographs or artwork, free graphics found on the Web, graphics already owned by the Website owner, or newly created by a graphic artist. Browsers commonly support the Compuserve Graphics Interchange Format (GIF) and Joint Photographic Experts Group (JPG) image file formats.

You Need to Know ✔

JPG images support a large number of colors and are therefore suited to photos. GIF images support fewer colors but can be animated, have transparent backgrounds, or be interlaced.

Multimedia and audio, video, and 3D productions can be made using a variety of software tools specifically designed for that purpose, and often require special *plug-in* software to be installed on the browser for proper display or playback.

Intellectual Property

The term *intellectual property* refers to property rights for ideas, concepts, and processes. Copyright law protects text, graphics, and other works of this type from misuse, except in a very narrow set of circumstances labeled *fair use*. Fair use is when the work is excerpted in a small portion for the purpose of example or criticism, or when it is considered simply a fact or set of facts.

Remember

Any work, as soon as it is produced, has copyright protection (whether or not the copyright symbol is attached to the work). Monitor the production of content so that copyrights will not be violated.

The ease with which material can be copied from the Web can make it difficult to verify the original author or creator of content. In effect, every work is suspect unless originally created by the developer or the developer's team.

Hosting, Loading, and Managing Website Content

When the initial production of Web pages and content is finished, the next task is to load them onto a Web server. Typically, the hardware is a computer (or load-balanced, clustered network of computers) that are specially designed and optimized for delivering Web pages and content to users.

Loading Web pages or creating them online can be performed in several different ways. For example, standard Web pages are easily loaded to a Web server across the Internet (from wherever they are created) using utility FTP programs. The FTP host address, username, and password for the Website must be known to make a connection.

Managing and maintaining Web content is the process of adding new pages, fixing errors, updating information, deleting information, and weeding out old pages. It is also frequently necessary to completely make over a site, both to upgrade the look and feel and to make the site more manageable.

Checking and Publicizing a Website

Like most software development, the design and construction of a Website usually involves errors and bugs.

You Need to Know ✔

With HTML, the bugs are often broken links and the errors are often misspellings or poor grammar, as well as poorly constructed HTML.

You can find HTML validation Websites by going to your favorite search engine and entering "Check HTML". You'll receive a list of sites that perform the service. Poorly constructed HTML can have hard-to-find consequences, depending upon the HTML editor and browser you are using. For example, accidentally leaving off an ending table tag causes no discernible effect if you are checking your work in Internet Explorer, but will cause the entire page to be blank when viewed in Netscape Navigator.

Publicizing your Website is an important step in letting potential users know the service is there. There are many kinds of publicity, including traditional marketing and advertising (radio, print, TV, direct mail, and so forth), but one of the most important and least costly is to register your site with search engines. The search engines will send requests to your site (using what's called *spider* or *crawler* software) and index the keywords on your site. Each search engine has different criteria by which they rate your site, and the criteria change over time. Your rating affects your place on the search engines for each keyword or search phrase used, and having a higher rating and placement can mean the difference between being found and being lost.

Chapter 2
HTML PAGE FORMATTING BASICS

The HTML Document Type Definition (DTD) and Elements

Every HTML document consists of a collection of elements. Every element begins with a starting tag containing the name of the element (<head>), and most elements conclude with a matching ending tag </head>. The line break element (<br>) is an example that contains no content and has no ending tag. Its function is to break a line at the point it is inserted.

A browser must know how to interpret these tags so there is a Document Type Declaration (DTD) corresponding to each element. Shown here is an example of the DTD for the line break element (<br>).

```
<!ELEMENT br  --O EMPTY  -- forced line break
     -->
<!ATTLIST BR
   %coreattrs;      --id, class, style,
        title-->
```

In the DTD, <br> is formally defined as an *element*, and it has a list of *attributes* (called %coreattrs;, for core attributes). While the DTD for elements can be very useful for advanced users, we will not usually specify them in this short introduction. We will provide a list of the most useful attributes for each element.

Writing Well-Formed HTML

In the official HTML 4.01 recommendation, there is a conformance guide that describes HTML tags with words such as MUST, MUST NOT, and REQUIRED to indicate how closely a particular directive has to be followed.

Also in the recommendation, you'll find tags defined as deprecated or obsolete. *Deprecated* means that the tag has become outdated, perhaps superseded by a newer element but can still be used and should be managed properly by browsers. *Obsolete* means the tag is no longer supported and there is no guarantee that a browser will render it effectively. Deprecated and obsolete tags should be avoided.

Attributes

An HTML element may have attributes or properties associated with it. These properties may have default values, and they may be assigned a value. For example, here is the syntax and attribute/value pair for setting the background color of a Web page to white:

```
<body bgcolor="#FFFFFF">
```

Legal attributes are defined in the HTML specification, and any legal attributes are included between the angle brackets (< >). They can be in any order. Generally, *attribute values are placed in quotes.*

 Important Point!

Attribute names are NOT case-sensitive, but the values assigned to them sometimes are case-sensitive.

The following image tag specifies the name of an image file to be inserted in an HTML document, and the file name is case-sensitive:

```
<img src="MyLogoFile.jpg">
```

Intrinsic Events

When a user requests a page, the document must first be loaded, and then the user is free to roam the document, clicking and double-clicking buttons and links, scrolling up and down, placing the mouse pointer over sections of text or images, or tabbing from field to field on a form. All of these actions are *events*, whose occurrence can be detected and used to trigger script actions. Triggering script actions is accomplished through the use of intrinsic events coded into beginning HTML tags. Many HTML elements support a variety of intrinsic events, such as *onload*, *onmouseover*, *onclick*, and so forth. The

descriptions throughout this book explain the events supported by each HTML element. Creating event-driven functions with scripting languages will be discussed in more detail in Chapter 7.

Character Entity References (Special Characters)

There are some characters that, if simply inserted into a plain text HTML file, would not display properly. The less-than sign (<), for example, would indicate to the browser the beginning of an HTML tag and would not be displayed. In order to force the display of these characters, *character entity references* (special characters) are used.

The syntax for displaying special characters is an ampersand, followed by either a pound sign (#) and the numeric value for the character or an abbreviation. It ends with a semicolon. For example, you could display a less-than sign with either of the following:

```
&#60;
&lt;
```

The characters that may be used in an HTML document are listed in the Universal Character Set (UCS), defined by ISO10646.

The Basic Structure of HTML Documents

HTML documents are made up of three parts: a line containing the *version information*, the *head* of the document, and the *body* of the document. Although browsers do not enforce it, technically HTML documents should start with a line indicating the DTD to be used (the version information). The DTD is contained within the <!DOCTYPE> element. An example of a common declaration is:

```
<!DOCTYPE HTML PUBLIC "-//W3C//DTD HTML 4.01
Transitional//EN">
```

The HTML 4.01 recommendation lists three DTDs that can be used for HTML documents, and they each include a reference to an online DTD file. The files contain information browsers may need to understand the documents. This line becomes very important when dealing with XHTML and XML. The three DTDs are:

```
<!DOCTYPE HTML PUBLIC "-//W3C//DTD HTML 4.01//EN"
"http://www.w3.org/TR/html4/strict.dtd">
<!DOCTYPE HTML PUBLIC "-//W3C//DTD HTML 4.01
Transitional//EN"
"http://www.w3.org/TR/html4/loose.dtd">
<!DOCTYPE HTML PUBLIC "-//W3C//DTD HTML 4.01
Frameset//EN"
"http://www.w3.org/TR/html4/frameset.dtd">
```

The *strict* DTD includes only elements and attributes that have not been deprecated and are not part of the *frameset* DTD. The *loose* DTD includes elements and attributes in the strict DTD as well as those that have been deprecated. The frameset DTD includes everything in the other two DTDs, as well as frames (discussed in Chapter 6).

The HTML Element

The HTML element is considered the root element of an HTML document, according to the DOM, and strangely enough both its starting and ending tags are optional, though rarely omitted. The opening HTML tag follows the DOCTYPE tag, if included, and all document content comes before the matching </html>.

The HTML tag can have two attributes: the *lang* attribute and the *dir* attribute. The *lang* attribute specifies the language of the document (using a two-character code for the country), and the *dir* attribute specifies the direction (left-to-right or right-to-left) in which text proceeds across the page.

The HEAD, TITLE, and META Elements

The HEAD tag marks the beginning of the document head element. Typically, nothing contained in the HEAD element is displayed to the user except the title. This element serves as a container for other elements (such as TITLE and META tags) and is optional (both starting and ending).

The TITLE Element contains the title of an HTML document, and both the starting and ending tags are required.

> # Remember
>
> An HTML document must have exactly one title. It will be displayed in the title bar of your browser.

META tags are not required, but can be included in HTML document head elements to provide information about the information contained in the page. A common use of META tags is to provide the keywords and descriptions pertaining to the page for search engine usage. For META elements, the starting tag is required but an ending tag is forbidden. The element itself consists of the definition of a property and a value. Coding a META element for a gift shop Web page might be as follows:

```
<meta name="keywords" content="gifts, birthdays,
Christmas, presents">
```

Some attributes of the META element are:

- *name* – The name of the property being established, such as keywords, description, and so forth.
- *content* – The value that is assigned to the property, such as a set of keywords, a short description, and so forth.
- *scheme* – The type of data contained in the value would be set (text is the default).

Here is an example of a typical Web page with HTML, HEAD, TITLE, and META tags:

```
<!DOCTYPE HTML PUBLIC "-//W3C//DTD HTML
4.01//EN"
"http://www.w3.org/TR/html4/strict.dtd">
<html>
<head>
<title>Here is the title of your page</title>
<meta http-equiv="Content-Type" content="text/
html; charset=iso-8859-1">
<meta name="keywords" content="first, second,
```

```
third">
<meta name="description" content="This is a de-
scription">
</head>
</html>
```

The BODY Element

The BODY element contains the major portion of Web page content that is actually visible on the screen in your browser. Within the BODY element you may insert text, images, links, tables, and forms, but not frames. The starting and ending tags are optional, although in practice they are almost never left out.

The starting BODY element tag can include several attributes such as:

- *background* – Specifies the location of an image file, which is then tiled across the background of the browser display area, starting at the top left. It is typically used to provide smoothly textured backgrounds for Web pages.
- *bgcolor* – Specifies a color for the background.
- *text*, *link*, *vlink*, and *alink* – All set a color for either text, hypertext links, links that have been visited (*vlink*), or links that are active (*alink*). Active links show their color when the mouse is over them and the left mouse button is pressed down.

All of the attributes above have been deprecated in favor of style sheets.

- *id*, *class* – These attributes apply to the BODY element (and also to other elements) and can be used to assign a unique name (*id*) to an element and to assign an element to a group (*class*). Once assigned a name or to a group, other tags can reference the element or group and apply styles or perform other selective functions.
- *lang*, *dir*, and *title* – The new attribute here is *title* which gives a title to its element. Think of *title* attributes as popup labels (such as you might see if you put your mouse over a link or image).
- *style* – This attribute specifies style information or an external style sheet for a page. (See Chapter 8.)

- *onload, onunload, onclick, ondblclick, onmousedown, onmouseup, onmouseover, onmousemove, onmouseout, onkeypress, onkeydown, onkeyup* – These are all events that the BODY element may be programmed to respond to by using a scripting language such as JavaScript.

Body Element Background Color

Adding color to the background of a Web page makes it much more visually appealing. The *bgcolor* attribute can also be used with tables, and setting the color values (discussed next) works the same for the *text*, *link*, *vlink*, and *alink* attributes of the BODY element.

Colors are specified in HTML using the Red, Green, Blue (RGB) color space. This means that colors are created using a combination of red, green, and blue color values from zero to 255 (a total of 256 values for each primary color, giving 256^3 or 16.7 million colors in all).

Color values are coded in HTML by setting the attribute equal to the hexadecimal value for the appropriate color, preceded by a pound sign, like this:

```
<body bgcolor="#FF0000">
```

In this example, the background color of the page would be pure red, because the hexadecimal value for 255 (FF) has been inserted into the first two characters of the color code, while the other values are set at zero. Most image-editing software programs provide decimal values for the colors red, green, and blue when you use their color picker functions. You must then convert the numbers to hexadecimal.

 **Note!**

Gray can be generated by any combination of color values in which the red, green, and blue color values are equal. Both of the following will produce a gray color but the first with be lighter.

```
<body bgcolor = "#111111>
<body bgcolor = "#EEEEEE">
```

Content within the BODY Element

All the content you wish to display to the user appears inside the BODY element of your HTML document. Text, images, forms, tables, and so forth appear on the screen in the order you write them.

Unless you are using absolute positioning, elements in an HTML document cannot appear to overlay each other, and they will start at the top left of the finished page, proceed from left to right across the screen until they run out of room, and then drop down to the next line. If there is enough content, a vertical scrollbar will appear allowing the user to scroll down the page, but a horizontal scrollbar won't appear unless you use tags to prevent line breaks or images or other objects wider than the screen width, since users hate to scroll horizontally.

Although you may make Web pages as long as you like, as a practical matter most pages should contain no more than three or four screens of content. If you do build pages that are longer, (e.g. catalog pages) make sure to provide some navigation mechanism so users can find their way around quickly.

In the HTML recommendation, browsers are referred to as user-agents, and user-agents as a class include a broad spectrum of software that is capable of rendering HTML documents in one format or another.

We are probably most familiar with the typical visual browsers, but there are user-agents that display only plain text, synthesize speech, or in some way or another radically change the output. HTML has mechanisms built in to accommodate some of this modification, and we should be aware of users who may not use a standard visual browser.

Visual browsers have a great deal of control over the display of content on Web pages. For example, browsers decide where to break lines and how to wrap words on a Web page. If you, as the user, change the size of the display screen window with your mouse, the browser will automatically try to re-wrap lines of text to fit the new screen size.

Remember

It is up to you as the Web page designer to ensure a pleasant, appealing, easy-to-navigate, and easy-to-download Website.

Block-Level/Inline-Level and Grouping Elements

Elements within the BODY element can be defined as block-level or inline-level elements. Think of *block-level elements* as larger structures, such as a whole section of a document, while *inline elements* may be a single image or paragraph.

In general, block-level elements may contain other block-level elements and inline elements, while inline elements may contain other inline elements and data such as text. Block-level elements typically begin on a new line, while inline elements remain on the same line unless there is not enough room on the screen for them.

The DIV Element and the Span Element

The DIV element creates a generic block-level element within an HTML document, meaning the author of the document can use the *id*, *class*, *lang*, and *style* attributes to set an effect for the block defined by the DIV element as a whole. The start and end tags are required.

In addition to the *id*, *class*, *lang*, and *style* attributes, the DIV element includes the *title* and *align* attributes. The *align* attribute can take on the values of *left*, *right*, *center*, and *justify*. The first three affect the horizontal placement of the element and the last, *justify*, means that both ends of a block of text will have even margins.

The DIV element can be used to trigger scripts when an event like *onclick* occurs.

```
<div align="right">
<p>Here is a paragraph. It will be aligned to
the right.
<p>Here is a second paragraph. It will also be
aligned to the right.
</div>
```

The SPAN element has the same attributes as DIV, and the same events affect it. The primary difference is that DIV defines a section of content as block-level, while SPAN defines a section of content as inline.

The ADDRESS Element

The ADDRESS element is sometimes used to supply contact information such as addresses, but is not used that frequently. The starting and ending tags are required, and the same attributes and events are allowed as for the DIV. Example:

```
<address>
John Doe
11223 Spring Street
San Diego, CA 92108
</address>
```

Using this element causes the address to be displayed in italics in Internet Explorer.

Text Formatting in Web Pages

In HTML, text formatting is performed by a combination of the tags used by the document author and settings within the user's browser. For example, unless line breaks are inserted by the author to force breaks at specific points, the author will not know where the line breaks are going to occur for any given combination of browser, screen size, and screen resolution.

You Need to Know

Browsers allow only one white space between words. If more white spaces are inserted within the HTML they are completely ignored, as are tabs, carriage returns, and line feeds. Additional white spaces can be inserted using the character reference * *.

The H Element (Headings 1–6)

The H element comes in a variety of sizes, starting with the largest (H1) and ending with the smallest (H6). A heading begins with a blank line, followed by the heading text and another blank line. The H element also sets the text in the heading to Boldfaced.

The starting and ending tags are required for a heading, and the same attributes and events as DIV and SPAN are allowed. For example, the following heading is large and aligned to the center of the page:

```
<h2 align="center">Welcome to My Page</h2>
```

 **Note!**

Headings are not measured in point sizes like ordinary text. When displayed in a browser H1 is very large, H2 is large, H3 and H4 are close to the size of standard text, H5 is small, and H6 is very small.

The Blockquote Element

The BLOCKQUOTE element is for defining a section of text as a quotation. Both starting and ending tags are required, and it allows the same attributes and elements as the block-level elements with the exception of the *align* attribute. BLOCKQUOTE elements are rendered as an indented block of text.

The SUP and SUB Elements

The SUP and SUB elements provide superscript and subscript formatting. Their starting and ending tags are required, and they support the same attributes and events as the BLOCKQUOTE element.
To produce 21st Century:

```
21<sup>st</sup> Century
```

Paragraphs and the P Element

Paragraphs are formatted in HTML using the P element. The ending tag is optional, if there is a starting paragraph tag at the beginning of the next paragraph.

When a P tag is placed on a line of text, it forces the browser to display a single blank line. The P element has the same attributes and events as the DIV element, and can use the *align* attribute to align text (*left*, *right*, *center*, or *justify*). It cannot contain other block-level elements, including other P tags.

Line Breaks and the BR Element

Since browsers control word wrapping, the BR element should be used in places when the author wants to force a line break. Only the starting tag is allowed. Other than the *id*, *class*, *title*, and *style* attributes, its only notable attribute is the *clear* attribute. This attribute indicates where text will continue if the text is next to a floating element such as an image (the default value is *none*, but the *clear* attribute can also assume the values *left*, *right*, and *all*). For example, if text is wrapping next to an image and the BR element is put in place in the middle of one of the lines, setting the *clear* attribute to *none* will make the text continue on the next line down, while setting the *clear* attribute to *left* will make the text continue below the bottom of the image.

Text Style Elements

Visually appealing text is enhanced by the use of bold, italics, underlining, teletype, and so forth. The HTML elements producing stylistic effects (B, I, U, BIG, STRIKE, TT, SMALL, and S) are not all deprecated, but the recommendation expresses preference for using style sheets to accomplish these effects.

These text style elements can be combined or nested, meaning, for example, that an author can place <i> tags inside <b> tags, like this:

```
<b><i>This text will be bold and
italicized</i></b>
```

Both the starting and ending tags are required. These elements can be modified using the standard *id*, *class*, *lang*, *dir*, *style*, and *title* attributes, and the standard events.

Lines and the HR Element

The use of a line across the page makes text more readable by breaking it up into easily discerned blocks. The Horizontal Rule (HR) element creates a line across the page, and essentially acts as a paragraph break, because even if it is set to extend only partially across the page (width = "50%", for example) it still pushes other elements off the line on which it resides.

The HR element has a required starting tag but a forbidden ending tag. It allows the standard *id*, *class*, *lang*, *dir*, *title*, and *style* attributes, and the standard events. It also allows the attributes *align* (the default is "center"), *noshade* (renders the line as solid instead of etched into the page), *size* (height in pixels), and *width* (length as a percentage). However, all these additional attributes are deprecated.

A Formatted HTML Page

Here is an example of a finished page demonstrating many of the elements we've covered. The resulting page is shown in Figure 2-1.

```
<html> <head> <title>The Title</title>
<meta http-equiv="Content-Type" content="text/
html; charset=iso-8859-1">
<meta name="keywords" content="text, formatting,
bold, italics, paragraphs">
</head>
<body bgcolor="#FFFFFF">
<h2>Welcome to the Example Web Page!</h2>
<p>Here is the beginning of a paragraph. Notice
there is no automatic indentation, and the words
wrap in the browser. To separate this section
from the next, we'll use a horizontal rule
(visible line with size = 10).
</p>
<hr size = "10">
```

```
<h3 align="center">Formatting and Alignment</
h3>
<p align="center">In this paragraph we'll apply
some formatting, such as <b>BOLD</b>,
<i>ITALICS</i>, <u>UNDERLINING</u>,
<tt>TELETYPE</tt>, <sup>SUPERSCRIPT</sup>,
<sub>SUBSCRIPT</sub> to demonstrate these
elements.
</body>
</html>
```

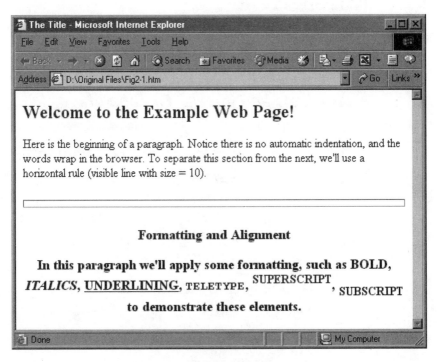

Figure 2-1 The demo page

Chapter 3
ADVANCED WEB PAGE FORMATTING

The FONT and BASEFONT Elements

HTML contains the FONT and BASEFONT elements for setting and managing font properties, and they are still widely used despite being deprecated in favor of style sheets.

Remember

The BASEFONT element establishes basic font properties for text on a Web page, while the FONT element sets font properties for a specific character, word, phrase, sentence, paragraph, or section of text.

The BASEFONT element does not have an ending tag. The following code sets the basic font size and face for a Web page. Notice that the BASEFONT tag is written just below the starting BODY tag of the Web page but before any FONT tags:

```
<html><head>
<title>The Title</title></head>
<body>
<basefont size="4" face="Arial">
This text is size 4 and displayed in the Arial
font face.
</body>
</html>
```

While the BASEFONT element only supports the *id* attribute as a core attribute, the core attributes of the FONT element are *id*, *class*, *lang*, *dir*, *style*, and *title*. Additional attributes supported for both elements are *color*, *size*, and *face*. The *color* attribute can be set using the RGB color-coding scheme discussed in Chapter 2, while the *face* is a comma-separated list for font face names such as Arial, Times New Roman, and so forth. The browser will search the user's computer for font faces, starting with the first in the list. If none of the listed font faces are found, the browser will use a default font.

The *size* attribute sets the size of the font on a scale from 1 to 7 with the actual screen size depending upon the screen resolution and how the browser interprets the size. The FONT element can set sizes directly, like this:

```
<font size="4">This text is size 4</font>
```

The FONT element can also set font size in relation to the BASE-FONT size, like this:

```
<font size="+2">This text is 2 sizes larger than
the BASEFONT size</font>
```

If the BASEFONT element is not used, the text size will default to 3.

Lists and the UL, OL, and LI Elements

Another useful text formatting technique is the numbered or bulleted list. HTML provides the UL element for *unordered* lists and the OL element for *ordered* lists. Both of these elements use the same basic structure to accomplish their tasks. They begin with 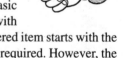 the <ul> or <ol> tag. Then each bulleted or numbered item starts with the <li> tag and may end with </li> although it is not required. However, the matching </ul> or </ol> tag is required.

These lists support the core attributes *id*, *class*, *lang*, *dir*, *style*, *title*, and the standard intrinsic events (*onmouseover*, *onclick*, and so forth). Other supported attributes (all deprecated) include:

- *type* – Allows the author to set the style of the symbol beginning the list item. For example, the UL element may have *type* set to "disc", "square", or "circle", while the OL numerical value may be rendered as number ("1"), alphabetical characters ("A" for uppercase and "a" for lowercase), or roman numerals ("I" for uppercase and "i" for lowercase). Some aspects of the rendering depend on the browser.
- *start* – Sets the starting value for ordered list items. While the

value is a number ("6", for example) the actual symbol rendered depends upon the setting of the *type* attribute (if the *type* value is "I" then a *start* value of "6" would produce VI in roman numerals).

- *value* – Sets the value of the current LI item, so that you can change numbering midstream. For example, if you wanted to jump from 3 to 12 in your numbered list you could do that by setting the *value* attribute to "12".

- *compact* – Tells the browser to display the list in a more compact way, but how it is rendered is up to the browser.

Definition Lists and the DL Element

A *definition list* is a structure for presenting terms followed by their definitions, with the definitions indented. This structure may be used in any case where the author wishes to present a single term or phrase followed by content related to the term, but the recommendation suggests using style sheets instead of this structure where the only desire is to produce indentation.

Within the DL element, the DT and DD elements produce the *definition term* and the *definition description*. Starting and ending tags are required for the DL element. Only the starting tag is required for the DT and DD elements.

No unusual attributes are supported, but the core attributes of *id*, *class*, *lang*, *dir*, *style*, and *title* are, as well as the standard intrinsic events. The following is the code for a series of lists. The result is shown in Figure 3-1.

```
<html><head><title>Lists</title></head>
<body bgcolor="#FFFFFF">
<p><font size="5">Unordered and Ordered Lists
</font></p>
<ul>
  <li>This is the first item in an unordered list
</li>
  <li>This is the second item</li>
</ul>
<ul>
  <li type="circle">Here is the circle</li>
```

```
<li type="square">Here is the square</li>
</ul>
<ol>
  <li>Here is an ordered list in numbers</li>
  <li>and the number 2</li>
  <li value="12">This number is different</li>
  <li>and this number follows the last</li>
</ol>
<p>Here is a definition list:</p>
<dl>
  <dt><b>Term 1</b></dt>
  <dd>The description for the first term</dd>
  <dt><b>Term 2</b></dt>
  <dd>The description for the second term</dd>
</dl>
</body></html>
```

Note that the bold font style for the definition list terms was added and is not part of the formatting of the definition list itself.

Preformatted Text and the PRE Element

To prevent the browser from ignoring additional spaces, the PRE element may be used. Following the starting PRE tag, the browser respects all white spaces, tabs, and so forth. Browsers will also render the text in a mono-spaced font such as Courier, and will prevent automatic word wrapping.

Both the starting and ending tags are required, and the PRE element supports the standard attributes such as *id*, *class*, *style*, *title*, *lang*, *dir*, and the standard events. The PRE element also supports the attribute *width*. This attribute specifies the desired width of the section (in number of characters), but is not widely supported.

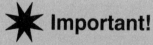 **Important!**

Elements such as IMG, OBJECT, SUB and SUP cannot be included in a PRE element.

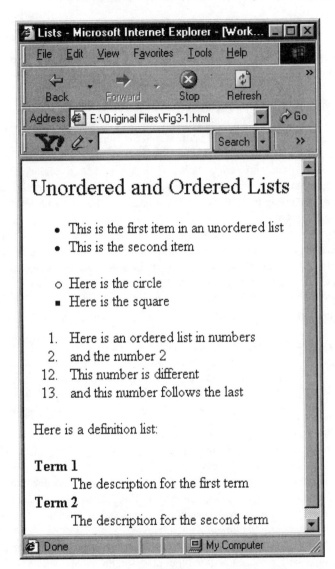

Figure 3-1 List Elements

HTML Hypertext Links

An extraordinarily powerful feature of HTML is the ability to connect directly to other documents or HTML resources by clicking content (for example text or images).

Within HTML the A (anchor) element serves to provide hypertext links, as well as several other useful features. Technically, the code providing the link to be clicked is considered the *source* anchor, and if there is code at the other document or resource providing a place to link to, it is considered the *destination* anchor. However, it is not necessary for anchor code to be present at the destination in order to complete the link. Simply including the URL of the destination within the source anchor code is enough.

Destination anchors use syntax similar to the source anchor, but must include a name. Names can be set with the *name* attribute. When a destination anchor is used, the name must be included within the source anchor URL. The following code shows source and destination anchors using the A element, including the *name* attribute at the destination. The last line is a destination anchor:

```
<a href="nextpage.htm">This text is clickable.
</a>
<a href="nextpage.htm#otherpagename">Goes to a
named anchor.</a>

<a name="otherpagename">
```

The first link is a common one having no destination name included. The page it refers to ("nextpage.htm") will appear in the normal fashion when the text message is clicked. Browsers render the clickable text blue and underlined, easily identifiable as a link. The second link includes the name of the destination anchor, "otherpagename". When the second link is clicked, the document named "nextpage.htm" will automatically scroll to the location of the named destination within the page. When creating links within a document to other places in the same document, simply including the pound sign and the destination name is enough to create a working link.

Although most links connect HTML documents to other HTML documents, it is possible to link to any file type. If the user's browser is capable, the file type will be opened. If not, the browser typically offers the user the opportunity to retrieve and save the resource to storage (such as a hard disk drive). In practice, this means users can open Web pages, image files, video and audio, multimedia, and many other common file types, without trouble. In addition, there are *plug-in* modules, freely available software that extend browser capabilities to open proprietary file types.

The A and LINK Elements

The A element is the most commonly used element for forming links to other resources on the Web. The LINK element, in fact, does not form links but instead provides information to the browser as to the author's intended relationship between documents. For example, the LINK element may be set to show which document is the previous page and which is the next page, as shown here:

```
<head><title>The Title</title>
<link rel="prev" href="page2.htm">
<link rel="next" href="page4.htm">
</head>
```

The starting tag for the LINK element is required but an ending tag is forbidden, and the LINK element may only be coded inside the HEAD element of a document. The standard attributes (*id, class, lang, dir, style,* and *title)* and the intrinsic events are supported. In addition, the following attributes are also supported:

- *charset* − Specifies the character set to be used to interpret the characters of the document being linked to.
- *href* − Specifies the URL of the resource being linked to.
- *hreflang* − Specifies the language of the document being linked to.
- *type* − Indicates the type of the content at the other end of the link. For example, there may be an audio file at the end of the link, rather than text.
- *rel* and *rev* − Indicate the relationship between the current and the target document, *rel* indicating the relation from the current

document to the target and *rev* specifying the reverse relationship. They are often used to identify the next and previous documents in a series of documents. However, their values can be any of the currently recommended link types, such as "alternate", "start", "next", "prev", "contents", "index", "glossary", and so forth. Their primary function is to assist the author with organizing content in a familiar, book-like, style.

- *media* – Intended to provide the browser information concerning what media the content is suitable for. For example, assigning the value "aural" to this attribute indicates the content is meant for speech-synthesizer.

- *target* – Can be used to specify the name of a frame in which to open the link. Of course, the author must give the frame a name in the code before a targeted link can be opened in it. Frames will be discussed in greater detail in Chapter 6.

Unlike the LINK element, the A or anchor element produces displayed links within an HTML document (or else a named anchor or destination that may be linked to).

The starting and ending tags are required for the A element (you'll know if you leave off the ending tag, because everything in your document will become clickable, in some browsers). The *id, class, lang, dir, style*, and *title* attributes are all supported, as well as the intrinsic events, quite a few other attributes, and two other events. They are:

- *shape* and *coords* – Used with client-side image maps, to be discussed in further detail in Chapter 5.

- *hreflang, rev, rel, target, type, and charset* – Same properties as in the LINK element.

- *name* – This attribute gives the link a name which is required if the link is going to serve as a destination anchor.

- *tabindex* – Specifies what element will be focused upon in what order as the user tabs through the document.

- *accesskey* – This attribute can be assigned a value equivalent to a key on the keyboard. The link will be activated when that key (or a key combination) is pressed

- *onfocus* – This event occurs when the element in question receives focus. *Focus* means the element is currently active upon the user's screen. For example, if a button has focus, it will have a dotted line around its caption on the Windows operating system.

- *onblur* – This event is the opposite of focus, and it occurs when an element loses focus.

Absolute and Relative URLs

Places on the Internet (connected computers, websites, and so forth) can be found using Internet Protocol (IP) Addresses. In IP version 4, IP addresses are made from a series of four numbers ranging from 0 to 255, for several billion possible combinations. Domain names map IP addresses to easy-to-remember names. Domain names and IP addresses are related to Uniform Resource Locators (URLs) in that the domain name or IP address of a Website is the second portion of a URL. URLs also contain other information allowing specific resources (files) to be found on the World Wide Web.

You Need to Know

URLs consist of four parts:

- The *protocol*, such as http.
- The *host computer name* or *domain name*, such as e4free.com, that represents the assigned IP address of the Website.
- The *path* to the resource, meaning the folder (and any subfolders) in which the file resides.
- The *filename* and *extension* of the resource.

Authors can use the entire or absolute URL to specify a resource within a hypertext link, or a relative URL. A *relative* URL takes its name from the fact that the resource is found by the browser relative to the location where the browser found the current document. For example, if only a filename is specified, the browser will assume the protocol, the domain name, and the path to be identical to those of the document currently being displayed, and it will attempt to find the file being linked to in the same directory. If a folder name is included in the *href* value, then the browser looks for the resource in a subfolder relative to the one in which the current document is found. Here is an example of absolute and relative *href* values:

```
<a href="http://www.e4free.com/mypictures.htm">
This is an absolute reference, and works from a
document located anywhere on the Web.</a>
<a href="mypictures.htm">This is a relative
reference, and works when the linked to document
is located in the same folder as the current
document.</a>
<a href="pictures/mypictures.htm">This is a
relative reference to a subfolder, and works
when the linked to document is located in a
subfolder named pictures beneath the folder of
the current document.</a>
```

The BASE Element

By default, the base URL from which relative links are calculated is the URL of the current document. If an author wishes to specifically set the base URL for a document, then this can be done with the BASE element. The BASE element must be placed in the HEAD element and must come before any other element that refers to an external resource. There is a starting tag for the BASE element, but an ending tag is forbidden.

The only attribute supported by the BASE element, *href*, can contain as a value an absolute URL. This URL becomes the base from which any relative URLs specified within the document are calculated, regardless of the actual location of the current document.

Placing Objects in Web Pages: the OBJECT and PARAM Elements

The OBJECT element is used to include various objects (for example a calendar displaying the correct date) in a Web page. These could be Java applets, but the OBJECT element is generic, meaning current and even future applications will have a mechanism by which they may be inserted into Web pages. The starting and ending tags for the OBJECT element are required.

The core attributes *id*, *class*, *lang*, *dir*, *style*, and *title* are supported, as well as the intrinsic events. The OBJECT element also supports the following attributes:

- *declare* – Allows the author to declare but not instantiate the object, and simply including the word *declare* in the tag performs this function (no value is set).
- *data* – Specifies the location of data used by the object. For example, if a calendar application loads appointment data for an individual, the value of the *data* attribute may be a URL pointing to the location where the data is stored.
- *type* – Specifies the content type of the data (such as text/html or image/gif) to be received from the location specified in *data*.
- *standby* – Can be set to a value that is displayed as a message while the object is loading.
- *classid* – Can be used to specify a location from which an object may be implemented, such as a URL.
- *codebase* – Similar to the BASE element, in that it specifies a base URL from which relative URLs may be calculated. For example, if the *classid* attribute is set as a relative URL, the *codebase* attribute will be used as the base URL from which to calculate the path to the *classid* location. If the *codebase* attribute is not set, then the base URL of the document will be used for this purpose.
- *codetype* – Sets the content type for data when the *classid* attribute is used.
- *archive* – Can contain a space-separated list of URLs of resources which may be used by the object, because some objects work with more than one data set.
- *tabindex* – Can be set to a number that specifies the order, in relation to other objects/elements on the page, to which focus will go as the user tabs through the page.
- *usemap* – Used with client-side image maps (discussed further in Chapter 5).
- *name* – Assigns a name to an object, so that it may be referenced by scripts and its contents submitted if it is within a FORM el-

ement (discussed further in Chapter 7).

- *align, width, height, border, hspace, vspace* – These attributes provide data for rendering the display of the object. They will be discussed in greater detail in Chapter 5, as they are used frequently with images.

These attributes help an object to be rendered properly and also to function correctly. For example, an object may need initial values applied when the object is first instantiated, or a stream of data to be processed.

Objects can be declared in the HEAD element if the author wishes, but authors should ensure that the object contains no data to be rendered because browsers generally don't render objects placed in the HEAD of a document. Objects declared in the HEAD element may be referenced by scripts, however, if they are assigned names via the *name* or *id* attribute.

Initializing Objects with the PARAM Element

Objects declared with the OBJECT element may be initialized with the PARAM element. Initialization means they are given initial operating values. For example, suppose a calendar object is included in a Web page. If the author wants a particular date displayed each time the calendar opens, then that date could be specified with the PARAM element. The value in the PARAM element could be a fixed date value, or it could be a location at which the current date (or some offset from the current date) could be found. The attributes of the PARAM element provide the capability to insert the appropriate data and tell the browser what kind of data is being provided.

The PARAM element has only a starting tag, and the ending tag is forbidden. Although the *id* attribute is supported, no other core attributes or events are. Additional attributes are:

- *name* – The parameter or property of the object to which the value will be given.
- *valuetype* – Indicates the type of value being supplied. If the *valuetype* is "data" (the default), the data in the *value* attribute will be evaluated and the result passed to the object as a string. If the

valuetype is "ref", then the *value* contains a URL pointing to a resource where the actual value or values are stored. Finally, if *valuetype* is "object", *value* contains the name of a declared object.

- *value* – Supplies the value for the property and is interpreted according to the type specified in the *valuetype* attribute.
- *type* – Specifies the content type ("image/gif", "text/HTML", and so forth) but is only used when the *valuetype* is set to "ref".

Here are just a few lines of code from a page constructed with Microsoft FrontPage 2000, using an ActiveX Control called the Calendar Control 9.0. It illustrates the insertion of PARAM elements.

```
<body> <object classid="clsid:8E27C92B-1264-
101C-8A2F-040224009C02" id="Calendar1"
width="288" height="191">
<param name="_Version" value = "524288">
<param name="_ExtentX" value="7620">
```

The APPLET Element

The APPLET element has been deprecated in favor of the OBJECT element, but since it is still in use it deserves mention here. The APPLET element is supported by Java-based browsers and is used for including Java applets in HTML documents.

The core attributes *id*, *class*, *style*, and *title* are supported (but only in the transitional DTD) and also the display attributes (*width*, *height*, *align*, *hspace*, and *vspace*). In addition, the *codebase*, *archive*, *code*, *object*, and *name* attributes are supported and perform similar functions as in the OBJECT and PARAM elements. The *alt* attribute is offered to provide an alternate means of displaying the presence of an applet for non-supporting browsers.

Chapter 4
WEB GRAPHICS
BASICS

IN THIS CHAPTER:

- ✔ *Web-Safe or Browser-Safe Colors*
- ✔ *Images and Image File Formats*
- ✔ *Creating Images*
- ✔ *Processing Images for the Web*
- ✔ *Inserting Images with the IMG Element*
- ✔ *Solved Problems*

Web-Safe or Browser-Safe Colors

Colors can be created on Web pages with HTML using either numeric values (in hexadecimal, such as #FFFFFF) or color names (see Table 4-1). Any individual browser recognizes hundreds of color names (although not always exactly the same ones, unfortunately). Web-safe (or browser-safe) colors are those that are supported by both Netscape Navigator and Microsoft Internet Explorer on either the Windows or Macintosh systems, when they are set to 256-color mode.

Table 4-1 Recommended color values and names

Black - #000000	Silver - #C0C0C0	Gray - #808080	White - #FFFFFF
Maroon - #800000	Red - #FF0000	Purple - #800080	Fuchsia - #FF00FF
Green - #008000	Lime - #00FF00	Olive - #808000	Yellow - #FFFF00
Navy - #000080	Blue - #0000FF	Teal - #008080	Aqua - #00FFFF

You Need to Know

HTML supports over 16.7 million colors, as defined by the RGB color scheme, but of these only 216 are supported by the major browsers.

Images and Image File Formats

Only certain image types are supported by browsers: Compuserve Graphics Interchange Format (GIF), Joint Photographic Experts Group (JPEG or JPG), and Portable Network Graphics (PNG).

Image file types suitable for the Internet are commonly compressed, meaning the file type takes up less space than the full-resolution original. For two of the supported image file types (GIF and JPEG) the compression is called *lossy* compression, because some data is lost when the image is converted to the supported file type. Because these image file types often appear much the same to the human eye, the data loss is acceptable and smaller file sizes mean faster downloads.

The Graphics Interchange Format (GIF)

The GIF format is useful because it compresses well and in more recent revisions of the format it supports interlacing, background transparency, and animation. *Interlacing* is the capability of the format to be broken into lines and transmitted across the Web, so that the image will begin to appear (as lines of gradually increasing sharpness) before all the data is received.

Transparent backgrounds are achieved by having the ability to designate a single color as having no color, and when this effect is applied to the background color, it makes the background appear transparent.

Animation is supported by the capability to incorporate multiple-image files into a single file, with playback data (such as file order, speed of frames, and so forth) included. Once the animated GIF file is created it can be inserted into an HTML page using the code identical to the code for inserting an ordinary image.

The JPEG Image File Format

The Joint Photographic Experts Group (JPEG) developed the JPEG image file format. As the name implies, it is suitable for photographic images containing many colors, and supports over 16.7 million colors (with 24-bit color). JPEG supports multiple compression levels, and the quality of the image depends upon the level of compression applied.

The PNG Image File Format

The Portable Network Graphics (PNG) image file format was developed in response to several needs: a more efficient format and a compression algorithm patent controversy associated with the GIF format. PNG uses *lossless* compression, and therefore image quality does not degrade during the compression process. PNG supports interlacing and transparency, but not animation. The PNG specification is considered to be stable and use of PNG is taking hold among technical users. Not all applications or browsers support all the features offered by PNG.

 **Note!**

Lossy compression refers to the loss of data when a file is compressed. While this is unacceptable for some file formats, for image files it is not only acceptable but required for practical use.

Creating Images

When an image is captured with a scanner, the images captured are called *raster* images, signifying that each pixel is assigned individual values. *Vector* images use equations to calculate the appropriate values for each part of an image. Raster and vector images are the two basic image types computers can use. Raster images record color and brightness data as pixels while vector images are mathematical representations of the lines and shapes making up an image. Raster images cannot be scaled well, and lose quality with significant scaling, while vector images scale quite well.

Images used in Web pages tend to fall into several distinct categories:

- Structural – Bars, backgrounds, buttons, arrows, and so forth. They assist the designer with page layout, look, and navigation. Clear, simple, unobtrusive buttons and backgrounds are usually better.
- Icons – Symbols that are meant to visually communicate information. Some icons convey their meaning easily to many people, but obscure icons should be avoided.
- Marketing – Trademark symbols, banner ads, logos, and other graphics that directly communicate a marketing message.
- Informational – Here the term refers to charts, graphs, flow charts, organization charts, and so forth. These graphics typically represent data, and may be static or dynamic (dynamic meaning the data from which they spring are changing, so that each user may see a different graphic).
- Photographic – Scanned or digitized photos. Thumbnail versions of photographic images let users decide which ones they wish to download.

Scanners

Scanners capture images in a format your computer and software can work with. Basically, scanning devices shine light on a subject and then focus that light on a sensor. The sensor reads the light values and records them as digital data, the familiar 1s and 0s. Inside the computer, image-processing software can be used to manipulate the scanned images and store the finished product as a file in an appropriate format.

Drum Scanners

To use a rotary drum scanner, artwork is affixed to a plastic cylinder (the drum) and then the drum rotates at high speed (over 1000 RPM in some cases) just a short distance from the sensing unit (which remains in a fixed, stable position). A very bright light source shines upon the artwork in a tiny spot, sampling the color and brightness values one pixel at a time.

Drum scanners can accommodate either reflective artwork (such as a photographic print) or transmissive media (such as a slide or negative) because they can produce light from inside or outside the plastic drum.

Flatbed Scanners

Flatbed scanners work by moving the light source and sensors past the artwork lying on a glass platen. A very bright light falls on the original and then is split into three-color channels using filters. The color and brightness values are converted into a stream of digital data by A/D converters and stored as a file in your computer.

Flatbed scanners can be divided into three categories:

- High-end – Approaching drum scanners in performance.
- Midrange – 600 dpi and up, 30 to 36 bit color depth.
- Low-end – 300 dpi, 24 bit color depth.

Film and Transparency Scanners

Without a good drum scanner, scanning films and transparencies requires a special transparency adapter for flatbed scanners. Such a scanner should accept at least 35mm slides and negatives, and better ones also accept other media sizes. Important characteristics to look for include special software and controls that make scanning negatives easier, as well as high optical resolution and excellent color depth and dynamic range.

Digital Cameras

A digital camera works just like a regular camera except the image is captured by a Charge-Coupled Device (CCD) after passing through the lens, rather than by a photo sensitive emulsion on the film. The primary advantage of digital cameras is the speed and ease with which they can take pictures, and that the images can be downloaded or erased quickly. The primary disadvantage is that they are more expensive than analog 35mm cameras and the resolution is somewhat lower.

Note!

Images can be produced using a drawing program, by scanning, and by taking a digital photograph. In each case the result is a file containing the digitized information.

Processing Images for the Web

The human eye can distinguish between millions of colors, all the subtle variations that make up the rich color spectrum we perceive. Color is actually electromagnetic waves (light) falling upon the retina after being focused by the eye's lens and stimulating special receptor cells in the retina. The resulting signal is transmitted to the brain by nerve cells. In order to accurately communicate color values to another person, color needs to be defined in an objective way.

Color Spaces

Color *spaces* (or color models) are used to describe color values in precise, standard terms. Computers and scanners use the Red, Green, Blue (RGB) color space, which is an *additive* system for reproducing color values. Additive systems generate color by transmitting light. For instance, computer monitors produce colors on the screen when electron beams cause the red, green, and blue phos-  phors to glow. The combination of the three colors in varying amounts displays the correct color. Colors produced using the additive process are always brighter than the colors that make them up.

Printers use the Cyan, Magenta, Yellow, and blacK (CMYK) color space, which is a *subtractive* system for reproducing color values. Subtractive systems generate color by absorbing some light and reflecting the rest. Colors produced using the subtractive process are always *darker* than the colors that make them up.

Because computers and scanners use RGB while printers use CMYK, and these color spaces do not overlap completely and are darker or lighter than their counterparts, the colors on a Web page will not look exactly the same when printed.

File Sizes

Higher-end scanners will allow scanning at a variety of color depths:

- 1 bit. Black and white (bitmapped or line art mode).
- 8 bit. Grayscale or indexed color mode.
- 24 bit. RGB color mode (8 bits in three channels).
- 32 bit. CMYK color mode (8 bits in four channels).
- 36 to 48 bits. High-bit RGB color mode (12 to 16 bits in three channels).

Obviously, a hard copy original will produce larger file sizes the more colors and channels are used to digitize the image. For example, a 48-bit RGB color mode file will be almost 48 times larger than the same original scanned at a 1-bit line art mode.

Remember

The term *resolution* refers to the amount of information contained in an image. Typically, people think of resolution as pixels, but formally it is the amount or density of digital information.

Pixels

The word *pixel* originally came from two words, picture and element. When you scan a photo, the colors and grayscales over the entire image are digitally sampled by separating the image into a pattern of dots, each dot being a pixel. The pixels in a raster image contain data about four properties:

- Size – The size of each pixel is directly related to the number of pixels scanned. For instance, if scanning at 300 dpi, a one-inch square of the image will produce 90,000 pixels, with each pixel being 1/300th of an inch on a side. Higher resolutions produce more pixels per inch, and each pixel is smaller. More pixels per inch means more data is being captured for the same image size, and therefore better detail and more continuous-appearing images are the result.

- Tonal Value – Tonal value is a function of the dynamic range of a scanner. With a small dynamic range, a scanner can only pick up a small portion of the visible spectrum. With a broad dynamic range, a scanner can pick up most of the visible spectrum. Regardless of how many colors the scanner can assign, a smaller dynamic range will produce less detail, because there will be less differentiation between the individual colors.

- Color Depth – Color depth refers directly to the number of colors that can be assigned to each pixel. If your scanner can only assign two colors (black and white, or 1-bit) your file sizes would be much smaller; with higher color depths the files would be larger.

- Location – Location data in a pixel refers to the X-Y coordinates of the pixel within a raster image. Each pixel has a location on the image, measured by the pixels themselves. A location of 5,5 means the pixel is located 5 pixels from the left (along the X axis) and 5 pixels from the top (along the Y axis).

Controlling Resolution

Resolution affects quality at every step throughout the scanning process. While it is important to ensure that scans are at a high enough resolution to get excellent quality in the end, it is also important to limit resolution to only what is really required. One thing affected by high resolution is file size, and files that are too large can be expensive and time-consuming to process, not to mention tougher to upload and download.

Here's an example of calculating file size for a typical scanned image (ignoring the overhead of location data and so forth). Assume the original image is 4 inches by 4 inches in size. Next, assume scanning at 300 dpi. Finally, assume scanning in RGB mode (3 colors). The calculations would proceed as follows:

$$[4'' \times 4'' \times (300 \text{ dpi})^2 \times 3 \text{ colors}] = 4{,}320{,}000 \text{ bits or over } 540\text{KB}$$

Note what happens when you increase the resolution to 600 dpi:

$$[4'' \times 4'' \times (600 \text{ dpi})^2 \times 3 \text{ colors}] = 17{,}280{,}000 \text{ bits or over } 2.16\text{MB}$$

Doubling resolution doesn't just double the file size, it quadruples it. The name for this phenomenon is geometric progression. Tripling the resolution will cause the file size to increase by a factor of nine. Clearly it's very important to know the proper resolution for the output quality you need, and scan at only that resolution.

Resizing Images

For display output (images to be displayed on computer monitors in Web pages, for instance), if the number of pixels in an image is changed, the size is changed. For instance, if an original that is 4 inches × 4 inches is scanned at 100 dpi, on a video screen it will appear 400 pixels × 400 pixels. The original size in inches doesn't matter, because the image's pixels will match those provided by the screen resolution. The same image scanned at 50 dpi will appear half the width and half the height (200 pixels × 200 pixels).

Don't Forget!

The best way to increase size is to increase the enlargement factor in the original scan.

Inserting Images with the IMG Element

The IMG element inserts an image into a Web page at the point in the code where it is inserted, unless the author uses x index, y index, and z index coordinates to place the image on the page. The major browsers with version numbers below 4.0 do not support the use of these coordinates.

The IMG element has only a starting tag; an ending tag is forbidden. The core attributes (*id*, *class*, *lang*, *dir*, *title*, *style*) and the intrinsic events are supported, as well as a few other helpful attributes. The *src* attribute value is the URL to the image file and can be an absolute or relative path.

One should always set the *alt* to a text message telling the user the contents of the image. Because users may have images turned off in their browser preferences (or may even be unable to display images if, for example, they are using a wireless device) an indication of the contents of an image can be very helpful.

The *border* attribute sets the size in pixels of a border around the image. This attribute is deprecated, and the default size depends upon the browser in use. Here is an example of the code for inserting an image and setting the *alt* and *border* attributes:

```
<img alt="Image of House" border="0"
src="ImageOfHouse.gif">
```

Solved Problems

Solved Problem 4.1

You have an image file containing 50 pixels per inch, measuring 1.5 inches by 1.5 inches. You have a requirement for the same image, but with a screen size of 3 inches by 3 inches. What can you do to achieve this objective? What will be the effect on the image quality?

Solution:

You can resize the image from 50 pixels per inch to 100 pixels per inch and this will double the size of the image on the screen. However, doubling is accomplished by interpolation, which adds pixels but adds no data. Therefore the image will most likely looked pixilated and probably be unsuitable for use. A better method would be to rescan the image at a higher resolution.

Solved Problem 4.2

You have a requirement to display an image that is quite large (in file size) on a Web page. What techniques do you have to display the image in a reasonable manner?

Solution:

One technique is interlacing, which means that the image is broken up and transmitted as lines that are gradually assembled in the browser. The effect looks as if the image is coming into focus. It takes just as long to download but seems faster and requires no special coding.

Another technique is the *lowsrc* attribute and includes a very low resolution image to be displayed first. Although it actually takes longer it can be more satisfying because the user gets a look at the complete picture quickly. Here is the code:

```
<img lowsrc="lowresimage.gif"
source="image.gif">
```

Chapter 5
ADVANCED WEB GRAPHICS

IN THIS CHAPTER:

- ✔ *Manipulating Images with IMG Element Attributes*
- ✔ *Image Alignment and Word-Wrapping*
- ✔ *Spacing Around Images*
- ✔ *Building Animated Graphics*
- ✔ *Introduction to Image Maps*
- ✔ *Solved Problems*

Manipulating Images with IMG Element Attributes

Although most image editing is done within the image-editing application of choice, HTML offers a few useful utility attributes within the IMG element to make editing easier and faster.

For example, the displayed width and height of images can be manipulated with the *width* and *height* attributes. If only one or the other of these attributes is assigned a value, the image is automatically scaled so that the ratio of height to width remains the same.

Both the *width* attribute and the *height* attribute can be assigned values in pixels or as a percentage of the screen. If a value of "50" is assigned, then the width or height is 50 pixels, but a value of "50%" means half of the screen.

 **Note!**

If an image or series of images takes longer to download than the HTML, the browser may render the page twice – once with broken image icons and again when the images arrive.

Image Alignment and Word-Wrapping

The *align* attribute is deprecated, but still in common use. Images can be aligned both horizontally and vertically. Aligning an image has an effect on surrounding text. While an image moves to the left side of the screen by default, setting the *align* attribute to "left" makes nearby text wrap around the image. The settings of the *align* attribute and their effects are as follows:

- "left" – Forces the image to the left and wraps the text (if any is near) around the image. Technically, the image is "floated" to the left, meaning it becomes part of the left margin, and text flows around the right side of the new margin as defined by the image. The *clear* attribute of the BR element controls where new lines start in text around "floated" images.
- "right" – Does the same as left (including the "floating" aspect), but with the image to the right margin.
- "middle" – Centers the image vertically on the text baseline (the text goes to the middle of the image).
- "top" – Places the image top vertically at the text baseline (the text goes to the top of the image).

- "bottom" – Places the image bottom vertically at the text baseline (the text goes to the bottom of the image).

The following code demonstrates the use of the *align* attribute of the IMG element and the *clear* attribute of the BR element. It is displayed in Figure 5-1.

```
<html><head> <title> Image Alignment </title>
     </head>
<body bgcolor = "#FFFFFF">
<img src = "dot_clear.gif" width = "200" align
     = "left"> A small transparent image which
     only contains 43 bytes has been inserted
     with a width of 200 pixels. It now takes
```

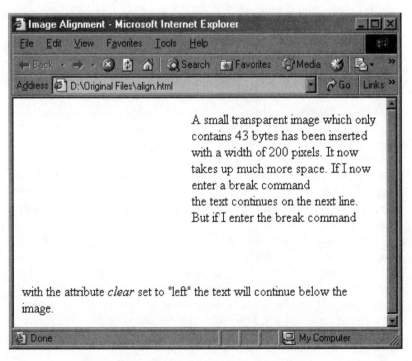

Figure 5-1 Positioning text around an image

```
        up much more space. If I now enter a break
        command
<br> the text continues on the next line. But if
        I enter the break command
<br clear = "left"> with the attribute
        <i>clear</i> set to "left" the text will
        continue below the image.
</body></html>
```

Spacing Around Images

Another device helpful in presenting images in a pleasing way is the use of horizontal and vertical spacing. Both the *hspace* and *vspace* attributes can contain numerical values for pixels, and if they are set, the number of pixels assigned is divided half on one side and half on the other. The effect produced is the inclusion of white space around the images.

Building Animated Graphics

The first step in the process of creating animated GIF image files is to decide the size the finished image is going to be. For example, a banner ad might be 300 pixels wide by 75 pixels high. Image-editing applications (like Microsoft Image Composer) allow the author to set these parameters before starting the image-building process. Next, the background color for the image should be chosen and set.

While it is tempting to start generating images immediately for an animated GIF, a prudent step is to storyboard the concept, to assist in the process of deciding what objects will be animated and how they will move from frame to frame. Text, clip art, drawn objects, and other components should be assembled and checked for color and size before inserting them into the working space.

Once a simple storyboard is complete and the components are in the working space, the author places them in their initial starting position and saves the first file. Each file is saved in the GIF image file format and numbered consecutively. From file to file the components of the animation are moved about, creating the illusion of motion in the finished product.

When all frames (files) have been created, a GIF animation utility program can be used to create the final animation file. Microsoft's Image Composer includes Microsoft GIF animator on the Tools menu. This utility presents a simple, button-driven interface that allows the author to insert GIF image files as a sequence of frames and then to modify the order, adjust playback attributes, and preview the animation. The finished product can then be saved under its own name. The saved file has a .gif filename extension, and is inserted into a Web page in the same way as any other image file.

Introduction to Image Maps

Image files consist of rows of pixels, and each pixel has a unique location on the user's screen. The browser can determine the location of a mouse click, and actions can be performed based on this location. An image map element allows regions of the image to be specified in the shape of circles, rectangles, and polygons. Common uses include actual maps or groupings of individual items.

Image maps work by providing the information that associates regions of an image with the action to be taken. The first image maps to be run depended upon *server-side* programs to direct the browser as to the action to take when a location on an image was clicked. Today the norm is *client-side* image maps in which the browser detects and processes the region coordinates instead of adding load to the server.

The *usemap* attribute must be included in an IMG element to turn it into an image map. It is set to the value of the name assigned to the MAP element. Figure 5-2 displays a small organizational chart.

Assigning Shapes and Coordinates to Client-Side Image Maps

The following lines of code are taken from the HTML page that produced Figure 5-2.

```
<body bgcolor="#FFFFFF" text="#000000">
<img src="OurCompany%20copy.gif" usemap="#tree"
     border="0">
<map name="tree">
  <area shape="rect" coords="20,192,94,223"
```

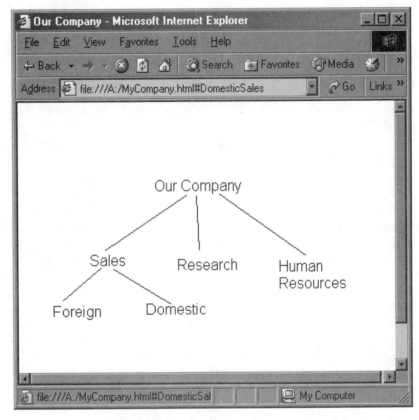

Figure 5-2 Image to be used with an image map

```
        href="#ForeignSales">
  <area shape="rect" coords="129,191,213,220"
        href="#DomesticSales">
</map>
```

Notice the *usemap* attribute in the IMG tag, which is set to the name of the MAP element that contains two AREA elements. The *shape* attribute of each indicates that it is a rectangle specified by the coordinates of its upper left and lower right corners. For example, the first rectangle has an upper left corner at (20,192) and a lower right corner at (94,223) positioned roughly over the word "Foreign." If the user clicks anywhere inside this rectangle, the browser will move to the named anchor given in the *href* attribute. The *href* could also hold the address of another Web page.

To make a circular image map region, only the center point and the radius are required. For example:

```
<area shape="circle" coords="314,86,14"
href="http://www.e4free.com/Ohio/">
```

The circle created by this code has a center that is located 314 pixels from the left side of the image and 86 pixels from the top of the image, and the radius is 14 pixels. Again, if the user clicks anywhere inside this circle, the browser will display the page given in the *href* attribute. The radius can also be calculated as a percentage of the smaller dimension. For example, if an image is 400 pixels wide and 300 pixels high, and the radius of a circular image map region is 20%, then the circle should have a radius of 20 percent of 300, or 60 pixels.

It is also possible to specify a polygonal region by expressing the coordinates of the vertices as x-y pairs for as many pairs as the author desires. The last pair should be the same as the first. The following example produces a four sided polygon.

```
<area shape="poly">
coords="142,231,94,154,201,198,175,236,142,231"
href=http://www.e4free.com/Hawaii>
```

A region may be set to no hypertext reference using the *nohref* attribute. Simply including this attribute in the element sets it, so there is no value to assign to it. With the *href* attribute, of course, the resource to which they will be taken is assigned as a URL. The *target* attribute allows the author to specify the frame in which to open the referenced document. The *alt* attribute is used to specify an alternate message for users (similar to the *alt* attribute for images) for an image map region, and the *tabindex* attribute is used to set the order in which image map regions are reached when the user tabs through a document. The *accesskey* attribute assigns a key (from the document character set) to a region, and when the key is pressed the hypertext reference will be followed.

A MAP element can contain multiple AREA elements each with its own *shape* and *href* attributes. When the mouse click occurs in one of the regions, the browser moves to the corresponding URL.

Note!

The easiest way to define an image map is to use an HTML editor such as Macromedia Dreamweaver or Microsoft FrontPage. Built-in tools allow the author to map the image visually and thus figure out the coordinates of the points.

Solved Problems

Solved Problem 5.1

Show the code that would make a client-side image map MAP element using AREA elements, in which there are five buttons, one each for About, Contact, Home, Order, and Privacy. Each button is 20 pixels high and 40 pixels long, and the buttons comprise the entire image. Use appropriate names for the links.

Solution:
```
<map name="NavBar">
<area shape="rect" coords="0,0,40,20"
href="http://www.e4free.com/About.htm">
<area shape="rect" coords="40,0,80,20"
href="http://www.e4free.com/Contact.htm">
<area shape="rect" coords="80,0,120,20"
href="http://www.e4free.com/Home.htm">
<area shape="rect" coords="120,0,160,20"
href="http://www.e4free.com/Order.htm">
<area shape="rect" coords="160,0,200,20"
href="http://www.e4free.com/Privacy.htm">
</map>
```

Solved Problem 5.2

An image 100 pixels high and 200 pixels wide is to be inserted into an HTML page with the *width* attribute set to 100. What effect, if any, will this have on the height of the image as displayed? On the file size?

Solution:

When only the width or height (but not both) is set, browsers automatically scale the other attribute so that the two attributes remain in the same ratio. In this case because the true width is 200 pixels, and the *width* attribute is set to 100 pixels, the height will also be scaled by a factor of one half to 50 pixels. The file size does not change.

Chapter 6
TABLES AND FRAMES

IN THIS CHAPTER:

- ✔ *Introduction to Tables*
- ✔ *The TABLE and CAPTION Elements*
- ✔ *Table Groupings and the THEAD, TFOOT, and TBODY Elements*
- ✔ *Column Groupings and the COLGROUP and COL Elements*
- ✔ *Table Rows and the TR Element*
- ✔ *Table Cells and the TH and TD Elements*
- ✔ *Creating Framed Web Pages*
- ✔ *The FRAMESET Element*
- ✔ *Retrieving Frame Content with the FRAME Element*
- ✔ *Targeting Frame Content*
- ✔ *The NOFRAMES Element*

Introduction to Tables

HTML tables allow authors to build columns and rows containing most of the other HTML elements and content. For example, text, images, links, forms, and even other tables can be included within table cells. To create a simple table, all that is necessary is the following code:

```
<table>
<tr>
  <th>Row 1, Column 1 Header</th>
  <th>Row 1, Column 2 Header</th>
</tr>
<tr>
  <td>Row 2, Column 1 Data Cell</td>
  <td>Row 2, Column 2 Data Cell</td>
</tr>
</table>
```

This code creates a table with four cells, the first two of which use the TH element to create table header cells. The use of the TH element denotes header information for a column or row and is rendered in a bold-faced font in most browsers, but otherwise has no unusual properties. The TABLE element, as shown here, is rendered as in invisible table with two rows of two cells each. The TR elements create the rows, and the TD elements create the last two cells in the table. By default, tables float to the left-hand side of the screen, and clear the line on which they reside of any other elements.

Remember

Invisible tables are still often used to provide a high degree of control over the placement of elements on Web pages.

The TABLE and CAPTION Elements

The TABLE element contains all the other elements that make up a table. For the TABLE element, the starting and ending tags are required, and the core attributes and intrinsic events are supported. The *dir* attribute works a little differently in the TABLE element, however, because setting it to "RTL" (the default is left to right) makes the table display columns from right to left. Only the TABLE element can have a reversed column order; individual table rows cannot.

Here is a summary of some of the attributes:

- *border* – Specifies the size of the border around the table. Set the *border* to 0 for no border.

- *summary* – Includes a text message summarizing the purpose of the table for browsers that don't support tables, such as speech-rendering browsers.

- *align* – Positions the table to the center, right, or left—left being the default.

- *width* – Can be set in pixels or as a percentage of the screen. If no width is specified, table sizing is a function of cell content sizes (images force cells to their size, while text wraps in the ordinary manner) and screen size.

- *bgcolor* – Sets the background color of a table using color codes or color names.

- *rules* – Specifies what lines of the border are visible. Setting the *rules* attribute to "rows"makes the browser show only horizontal lines. May be set to "none", "groups", "rows", "cols", and "all". The default is "all".

- *frame* – Specifies which of the exterior sides of the table will be visible. The permissible values for *frame* are:

    "void" – No sides are shown (the default value).

    "above" – The top side is shown.

    "below" – The bottom side is shown.

    "hsides" – The horizontal sides are shown.

    "vsides" – The vertical sides are shown.

    "lhs" – The left-hand side is shown.

    "rhs" – The right-hand side is shown.

    "box" – All four sides are shown.

    "border" – All four sides are shown.

- *cellpadding* – Defines the amount of space between the content of a cell and the inside edge of the cell.
- *cellspacing* – Specifies the spacing between cells, pixels, or as a percentage.

The CAPTION Element

The CAPTION element allows the author to provide a short description of the table (a caption). However, it is deprecated, and is not supported by all browsers. The CAPTION element may only appear immediately following the starting TABLE tag, and both the beginning and ending tags are required.

The core attributes and intrinsic events are supported as usual. The only other attribute for the CAPTION element is the *align* attribute. This forces the caption to the top, left, or right (at the top), or to the bottom of the table. To set a caption at the top right of a table, the syntax is:

```
<table>
<caption align="right"> The caption goes here
</caption>
the rest of the table tags and content follow
```

Table Groupings and the THEAD, TFOOT, and TBODY Elements

Tables, like other common document formats, are more useful when sections can be *grouped* according to function. The purpose of the THEAD, TFOOT, and TBODY elements is to allow such grouping for the TABLE element. Depending upon the browser used, these elements may be rendered at the top, in the middle, or at the bottom of the table, and can be treated as a group for the purposes of setting styles, as well as being independently scrollable. Internet Explorer appears to properly support these elements, but not Netscape Navigator.

Starting tags are required for these elements, but ending tags are optional. Each section must contain at least one row (defined by TR tags) and all should contain the same number of columns.

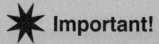

Important!

The TFOOT element should appear before the TBODY element.

The TBODY element is required except where there is only one TBODY section and there are no THEAD or TFOOT sections (as in the case of a standard table).

The core attributes and intrinsic events are supported, as well as two other interesting attributes, *cellhalign* and *cellvalign*. These specify alignment of content within the rows/cells of the section in which they appear, and can take on typical alignment values such as "left", "center", "right", "justify", and "char" (horizontal), and "top", "middle", "bottom", and "baseline" (vertical). Following is an example of the code that might be used to create a table with sections (shown in Figure 6-1):

```
<html><head><title>Untitled document </title>
   </head><body>
<table rules="cols" width="75%" border="1"
   frame="hsides">
<caption align="bottom">This is the caption
   </caption>
<thead>
<tr><td colspan=3>This is the Table Header
   Section</td></tr>
</thead>
<tfoot><tr><td colspan=3>This is the Table
   Footer Section</td></tr>
</tfoot>
<tbody>
   <tr><td> </td><td> </td>
   <td> </td></tr>
</tbody>
<tbody>
   <tr><td> </td><td> </td><td> 
   </td></tr>
</tbody>
```

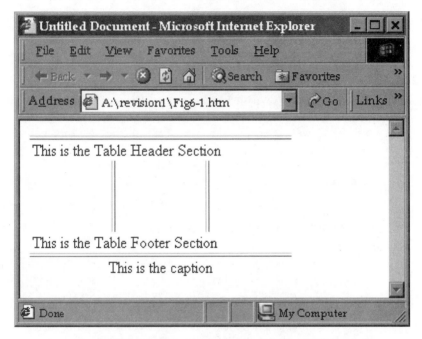

Figure 6-1 Table with THEAD, TFOOT, and CAPTION attributes

```
<tbody>
   <tr><td> </td><td> </td>
   <td> </td></tr>
</tbody>
</table></body></html>
```

Column Groupings and the COLGROUP and COL Elements

A table created without COLGROUP elements contains a single, implicit COLGROUP element, while a table with explicitly defined COLGROUP elements allows the author to define structural divisions within the table as column groupings. These groups of columns may be assigned style attributes using style sheets (more on style sheets in Chapter 8) or

HTML attributes (for example, the *rules* attribute). In contrast, the COL element allows the author to assign attributes across one or more columns without implying any structural grouping.

If a table contains any COLGROUP or COL elements, their span attribute values will be used to calculate the number of columns to render; if none are found, the row with the most cells will determine the number of columns in the table. Any rows containing less than the maximum number of cells will be padded with empty cells (on the right for a left-to-right table and on the left for a right-to-left table).

A starting tag is required for the COLGROUP element, while the ending tag is optional. Once again, the core attributes are supported, as well as the intrinsic events. Here is a summary of some of the attributes:

- *span* – Specifies the number of columns to which the COLGROUP element refers. The default value is 1.
- *width* – Specifies the width of columns within the COLGROUP element in terms of pixels, percentage, relative values, or a special zero asterisk (0*) value. Examples: "40" means the column is 40 pixels wide; "20%" means column is 20 percent of the width of the entire table. Columns in a COLGROUP element with a *width* attribute assigned a numerical value followed by an asterisk (such as " 2*, 3*,5*") will be given width according to the relative value of their assigned number, in this case 20 percent, 30 percent, and 50 percent of the available table width. The zero asterisk ("0*") value tells the browser to give only enough room to each column to contain its content.
- *align* – May have values of "left", "center", "right", "justify", and "char".
- *char* – Specifies a character from which alignment will proceed backwards and forwards in a column of text. For example, if a column contains currency values, then the assignment, char=".", will line up all values by the period.
- *charoff* – Specifies the amount of offset from the margin to the alignment character.
- *valign* – Specifies vertical alignment of content within cells as "top", "middle", "bottom", and "baseline".

Here is code used to establish a variety of columns:

```
<html><head><title> Column Example
    </title></head>
<body><table width="90%" border = "1">
<colgroup span = "3" width = "300" valign =
    "top" >
<colgroup span = "2" width = "100" valign =
    "bottom">
<tr>
  <td> Column 1 has a little data to
      display</td> <td>Column 2 has less</td>
  <td> Column 3 takes a little bit more
      space</td> <td>Col 4 </td>
  <td> Col 5 </td>
</tr>
</table> </body> </html>
```

The result is shown in Figure 6-2. Notice that the first three columns that form the first group are wider and the text is aligned at the top. The second group has narrower columns and the text is aligned at the bottom of the cell.

The COL elements can be placed inside COLGROUP elements to specify properties of individual columns within a group. It has the same attributes as the COLGROUP element.

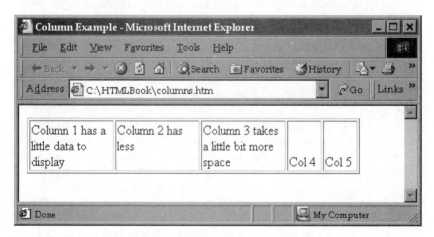

Figure 6-2 Using COLGROUP

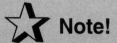

Note!

The *width* attribute of the COL element overrides the *width* attribute of a COLGROUP element in which it is contained.

Table Rows and the TR Element

Table rows are initiated with the TR element, whose starting tag is required but whose ending tag is optional. Within the TR element can be placed TH and TD elements, creating cells in a row. As we have mentioned, if the number of cells (including cells spanning more than one column) in a row is less than the total number of columns, blank cells will be added to that row until the total number of columns is reached.

The core attributes are supported, as well as the intrinsic events, and in addition to the cell alignment (*align*, *cellhalign*, *cellvalign*, and *valign*) attributes and text alignment (*char* and *charoff*) attributes, the TR element also supports *bgcolor*, allowing the author to specify a background color for an entire row. If the author omits COLGROUP and COL elements, by default the highest number of cells in any row becomes the total number of columns for a table.

Table Cells and the TH and TD Elements

Table cells are containers for data and content within tables. While cells may be empty, and may show either as a raised surface, or as an empty, indented cell, they typically contain data. However, data is not all they can contain. Text, images, links, forms, and form elements, and even whole tables can be placed into a table cell. Table cells cannot be smaller than the minimum size for the content they contain. Starting tags for the elements are required, while ending tags are optional.

The core attributes and intrinsic events are supported. If a cell is meant to be rendered as spanning a number of rows or columns, the *rowspan* or *colspan* attribute may be set. These attributes take as a value an integer representing the number of rows or columns to be spanned. The default value is 1. If their value is set to "0" then the cell will span whatever rows or columns remain.

Remember

The *width* and *height* attributes recommend width and height to the browser, but no cell can be smaller than its content.

The *cellhalign* and *cellvalign* attributes operate in the same way they do for TR and COL elements.

Set the background color with the *bgcolor* attribute. The following is an example of code that creates several cell types. Figure 6-3 shows how this code displays in a browser.

```html
<html><head><title>Table Cell Demo</title>
</head>
<body bgcolor="#FFFFFF">
<table width="90%" border="3">
    <tr> <td width="35%"> </td>
        <td width="18%"> </td>
        <td rowspan="2" valign="top"
          width="47%">
        <div align="center">Text at
          Top</div></td></tr>
    <tr>
        <td colspan="2" bgcolor=
          "#99CCFF">  </td></tr>
    <tr>
      <td height="60" width="35%"> </td>
      <td height="60" width="18%"> </td>
      <td height="60" width="47%"></td> </tr>
</table></body></html>
```

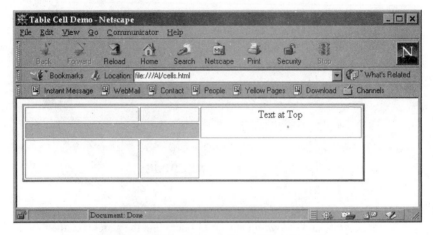

Figure 6.3 Illustration of a table with cells

Creating Framed Web Pages

Web pages containing frames are actually several Web pages displayed together in a framed format. The initial Web page retrieved is the framed page itself, and its primary function is to render the frames in which subsequent Web pages appear. Within the code for the initial framed page are references to other pages that appear in each frame. These are normal Web pages, but only the portion of their content that fits within the frame in which they appear is displayed. Of course, if the author chooses to allow scroll bars, users can scroll to reveal other content within the Web pages appearing inside the frames.

An advantage of using frames is that multiple pages can appear in the same frame, preserving the look, feel, and layout over the overall framed page as Website content is navigated. For example, one banner and one navigation page can constantly be available to the user (typically in the top and left frames, respectively). Not only does this make it easier to navigate the Website, but the pages and code for these areas of the page need be written and maintained only once, rather than over and over again for each page in the Website.

The drawback is that a significant number of users have still not upgraded to browsers that are frames compatible, and these browsers may display little or nothing to the user when a framed page is encountered.

However, the NOFRAMES element allows authors of framed pages an option for providing content to browsers that do not support frames.

The FRAMESET Element

From a structural standpoint, framed pages are different from standard pages in that they have HEAD and FRAMESET elements, rather than HEAD and BODY elements. In addition, while a standard page can have only one BODY section, a framed page can have multiple FRAMESET elements.

The recommendation does not appear to in-dicate whether starting and ending tags are re-quired, but it is a good idea to include them. Only the *id*, *class*, *title*, and *style* core attributes are supported, and only the *onload* and *onunload* events are supported. Other supported attributes are *rows* and *cols*. These two can be used simul-taneously, but often only one or the other is used. If a FRAMESET element uses the *rows* attribute, then the window of the browser will be broken into rows (initially); us-ing the *cols* attribute breaks the window into columns. Using both attri-butes in the same FRAMESET element creates a grid.

The row or column values may be expressed as pixels, percentages, or relative values. Each type of value can be used for a similar effect, as shown in the following three code examples. In each example, a FRAME-SET with four frames in columns covering one-quarter of the window is created.

Using *percentage value*:

```
<frameset cols="25%,25%,25%,25%">
```

Using *pixels* (with a screen resolution of 800 pixels wide):

```
<frameset cols="200,200,200,200">
```

Using *relative values*:

```
<frameset cols="2,2,2,2">
```

When rendered, frames start at the left and proceed to the right (if columns) and start at the top going down (for rows). If both rows and columns are used in the same FRAMESET, the order is left to right, top to bottom, essentially the same. FRAMESET elements inside FRAME-SET elements are called *nested* frames.

Retrieving Frame Content with the FRAME Element

While the FRAMESET element lays out the spaces for frames within a framed Web page, the FRAME element does the work of retrieving content pages for each frame, as well as some formatting of individual frames. For example, the FRAME element controls resizability and scrolling characteristics for frames.

No ending tag is required for the FRAME element. The core attributes *id*, *class*, *title*, and *style* are supported, but no events. The most important attribute is the *src* attribute. The *src* attribute defines the URL from which the Web page displayed in a frame is retrieved.

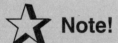 **Note!**

The URL must not be an anchor within the same page as the FRAMESET page. All content for frames must be from separate Web page files.

Other useful attributes include:

- *name* – Used to identify the frame so that when a link elsewhere on the page is clicked the desired page can appear in this frame. By default, links appear in the frame in which they are clicked, but if they are targeted to a named frame they will appear in that frame. (See "Targeting Frame Content.")
- *noresize* – If present, instructs the browser not to allow the user to resize the frame.
- *scrolling* – Controls the appearance of scroll bars, and may take

one of three values: "auto", "yes", and "no". The default is "auto", meaning that scroll bars will appear if the content will not fit in the frame boundaries.

- *frameborder* – Setting *frameborder* to "0" means that no frame borders will appear for this frame. Setting it to "1" (the default) means there is a border.
- *marginwidth and marginheight* – Defines the number of pixels between the content of a frame and its margins. The browser determines the default value.

The following code shows a simple nested frameset page, with frame names, content sources, and a few extra attributes that are not part of the recommendation. It is displayed in Figure 6-4.

```
<html><head><title>Nested Framesets and Frames
</title></head>
<frameset rows="20%,80%" frameborder="1"
```

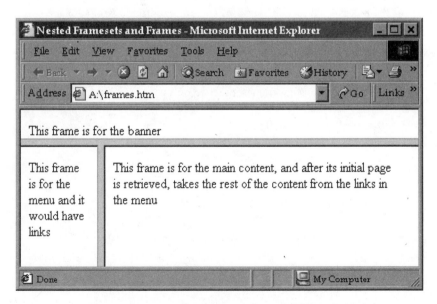

Figure 6-4 A nested frameset page, with borders

```
border="6" framespacing="6"
bordercolor="#FFCCCC">
   <frame src="Frame4.htm" name="banner" noresize
scrolling="no">
<frameset cols="20%,80%">
   <frame src="Frame2.htm" name="menu" noresize
scrolling="no">
   <frame src="Frame1.htm" name="main" noresize >
   </frameset>
</frameset>
<noframes><body bgcolor="#FFFFFF">
</body></noframes></html>
```

Targeting Frame Content

A very useful feature of frames is the ability to display content in one frame based on links activated in another frame. In order for this to work, the page in which the link appears must have a means of specifying the frame in which the retrieved content is to be rendered. The *target* attribute of the link is used for this purpose. The *target* attribute works for links, image maps, and forms. The value taken by the *target* attribute is the name assigned to that frame, via the *name* attribute of the FRAME element. Following is an example of a frameset file in which the frames have names, and a catalog file in which the links have assigned targets.

In the frameset file (frameset section only):

```
<frameset cols="50%,50%">
<frame src="page1.htm" name="Page1">
<frame src="page2.htm" name="Page2">
</frameset>
```

In the page1.htm file (link section only):

```
<a href="page3.htm" target="Page2">Link to Page
3</a>
<a href="page4.htm" target="Page2">Link to Page
4</a>
```

This is a common pattern in which the first frame is used as a navigation bar, holding links to other pages that will be opened in the second frame.

Remember

If no target is set, a link will open in the frame in which it resides.

The NOFRAMES Element

If a browser supports frames, it will ignore the contents of a NOFRAMES element. Thus the NOFRAMES element provides a place to insert content for browsers that do not support frames. Accordingly, a normal BODY element and any other ordinary content may be inserted into this space and it will be ignored by a frames-capable browser. Browsers unable to support frames will, in turn, ignore all FRAMESET and FRAME elements, and see only the content between the NOFRAMES element tags.

The following code shows how the NOFRAMES element is used to display information to older browsers that do not support frames:

```
<noframes> <body>
<p>This page uses frames, but your browser
doesn't support them.</p>
</body></noframes>
```

Chapter 7
WEB PAGE FORMS

Web Page Forms and the FORM Element

Forms have been included with HTML almost since the beginning, primarily because they offer such a valuable capability to Web page authors: the potential for users to communicate directly back to the author. The purpose of forms, of course, is to collect individual pieces of information.

HTML forms all start with the starting form tag and end with the ending form tag. Form submission, via the submit action, occurs when the user activates the submit action, usually by clicking a submit button. When a form is submitted, the browser typically sends the names and values of form controls back to the server on which the Website resides, often for further processing.

FORM elements can contain all the ordinary HTML elements, such as text, images, tables, hypertext links, and so forth. These elements are useful for creating a pleasant layout and design for the form, as well as labeling each INPUT element for the user. Text boxes, radio buttons, submit buttons, and so forth are called *controls*, and their appearance is pretty well fixed, unless special controls (OBJECT and BUTTON elements, for example) are used. Each control must be individually named (via the *name* attribute), so the author (and any scripts that might have an action required) can determine the control to which a particular value is associated.

The core attributes and intrinsic events are supported. Other important attributes include:

- *action* – The URL of the script or application responsible for processing the contents of the submitted form.
- *method* – Specifies the HTTP method by which form contents are submitted. It can be set to "GET" (the default value) or "POST" (the most common). Using the "GET" method makes the browser attach the name-value pairs of the form to the URL request sent to the server, while using the "POST" method makes the browser send the name-value pairs in the body of the form.
- *name* – Enables scripts to refer to the form by this name.

The additional events are *onsubmit* and *onreset*. These events are activated whenever the *submit* or *reset* methods are performed.

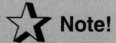

Note!

Authors commonly use the *onsubmit* event to trigger JavaScript processing that checks the contents of form controls to make sure that required fields contain new values and to validate the values entered.

The following example shows the construction of a very simple form for entering and sending an email address back to the server:

```
<form method="POST"
    action="collectemailaddresses.asp">
    Please enter your email address here:
    <input type="text" size="40"
        name="emailaddress"><br>
    <input type="submit" value="send">
</form>
```

In the example given, notice that the *action* attribute specifies an Active Server Page (ASP) that is in the same folder as the form. This means when the submit button is clicked the browser will send the contents of the form back to that ASP for processing. The script may perform some processing on the value and return information to the user; it may place the email address in a text file for later retrieval by the author; or it may put the email address into a database for subsequent use. HTML allows data to be retrieved from the user via forms, but almost anything is possible once the data gets back to the server for processing by a script or program.

You Need to Know ✔

The *action* attribute of the FORM element specifies the URL to which form contents are submitted. Often, this URL points to a script on the Web server where the Website resides. The script may be ASP, CGI scripts, executable applications, and so forth. The data is sent when the "submit" button is clicked.

Handling User Input with Form Controls

HTML form controls come in a variety of useful types. For example, there is the plain text box, in which users can enter text such as a name or a phone number. There are also radio buttons and checkboxes, equivalent to yes/no fields; SELECT elements that display as dropdown menus; and text areas that form larger boxes for entering multi-line data. And of course there are submit and reset buttons for submitting the contents of a form or resetting the form to its original configuration. Because the data sent back to the server consists of name-value pairs, the author of a form should give each control a unique name.

Controls have both an *initial value* and a *given value*. When the form is first loaded the *initial value* (which may be nothing) is assigned, while the user or scripts may change this value to a *given value*. Whatever value is currently assigned to the control is called its *current value*, but if a form is reset, it reverts to its *initial value*.

When a form is submitted, controls for which a value is assigned are combined into a name-value pair string and sent back to the server. However, while there may be many controls on a form, only those that have a properly assigned current value are included, and these controls are said to be "successful." For example, in the case of radio buttons, only a selected radio button is submitted. The other buttons are "unsuccessful." If several checkboxes of the same group (having identical names) are checked, their values will be returned as a comma-separated list paired with the single name of the group.

The INPUT Element

INPUT elements begin with a required starting INPUT tag and have no ending tag. The core attributes and intrinsic events are supported, as well as a wealth of other attributes specifically designed to make HTML forms highly functional user input devices. Here are some of the values for the attribute *type*:

- "text" – Creates a single line of text entry.
- "password" – Creates a text box in which entered data is displayed as asterisks, therefore shielding the actual data entered from prying eyes.
- "radio" – Creates a single radio button within a group, only one of which can be selected.
- "checkbox" – Creates a single checkbox within a group, all of which can be selected.
- "submit" – Creates a button that submits the form contents.
- "reset" – Creates a button that resets the form controls to their initial values.
- "button" – Creates a push button that may be manipulated by scripts.
- "image" – Uses an image as a submit button.

The default value for an INPUT element's *type* attribute is "text". The *name* attribute assigns a name to an INPUT element, and the *value* attribute, if assigned, gives the element its initial value.

If radio buttons or checkboxes are assigned the same name, they become part of a group. In the case of radio buttons they are mutually exclusive (typically used for choosing among credit card types). Checkboxes, on the other hand, while not mutually exclusive, will return a comma-separated string of values, one for each checkbox chosen from the group.

For INPUT element text boxes and password controls, the *size* attribute specifies the size of the box displayed, while the *maxlength* attribute specifies the maximum length of data (in characters) that can be entered. For INPUT elements of type "image", the *src* attribute specifies the URL of the image used.

The *tabindex* attribute can be set with a numerical value (some integer) in order to specifically assign a tab order to a form. When a form is loaded a tab index is assigned automatically, but it is often useful in the case of complex forms to assign a tab order explicitly. The exact numbers you use for values of *tabindex* are not important—only their order. If three controls had *tabindex* values of 1, 5, and 7, they would be visited in exactly the same order as if they had the values 2, 4, and 6.

You Need to Know

If *tabindex* values are assigned with numbers like 10, 20, 30, it is easy for an author to insert new controls without renumbering each time.

If an author uses the *accesskey* attribute, a key can be assigned that brings focus to a form control. *Bringing focus* usually means the same thing as clicking on the control. For example, for a text box it means that the user will be able to enter text, but does not actually place any text in the control. For a radio button, on the other hand, bringing focus usually means that the button will be selected.

Focus is also involved in the *onfocus, onblur, onselect,* and *onchange* events. When a control receives focus, the *onfocus* event activates, and can be used to trigger scripted actions. Likewise, when a control loses focus, the *onblur* event fires. In a similar manner, when text is selected in a control, the *onselect* event is triggered, and when a change is made to the value of a control the *onchange* event fires. All of these events can be used to trigger processing by scripts and therefore changes in the page being viewed by the user in real-time.

The following code sections provide examples of an abbreviated but workable form including many of the controls and attributes discussed so far, with a table arranging controls nicely on the page.

To start the form:

```
<html><head><title>Registration</title></head>
<body>
<form method = "POST" action="register.asp">
```

Notice the method attribute is set to "POST" and the action attribute is set to return the results to a file that is designated an ASP script by its extension.

To start the table that holds the contents of the form together:

```
<table width="100%" border="0">
<tr bgcolor="#CC9966"> <td colspan="2">
  <p align="center"><b><font size="+1"
    color="#FFFFFF">REGISTER HERE </font> </b>
    </p> </td></tr>
<tr bgcolor = "#FFCC99"> <td colspan= "2">
  <p align= "left" ><b>
<font color="#663333" size = "+1"> PLEASE FILL
    IN CONTACT DATA </font> </b> </td></tr>
```

The purpose of this form is to take registration information from potential buyers and suppliers. In practice there would be many more fields on the form. The first INPUT element is a radio button so the script can identify the type of user registering as either a Buyer or Supplier.

```
<tr bgcolor = "#FFCC99">
<td align = "right" width = "39%">
<div align = "center"> <b> I am a Buyer
<input type = "radio" name = "BorS" value =
    "Buyer" checked> Supplier
<input type = "radio" name = "BorS" value =
    "Supplier">
</b> </div></td><td width= "61%"></td></tr>
```

The *checked* attribute is present in the first of the radio buttons. The first radio button will be checked when the form is loaded, but clicking the other button will uncheck the first. Notice the names of both radio buttons are identical. No matter where on the form these two attributes are placed, they remain part of a group, connected by name, and only one will be successfully submitted.

To start the first fill-in section for ordinary contact information:

```
<tr><td width="39%" align = "right"><b>
First and Last Name:</b> </td>
<td width = "61%"> <input type = "text"
     name="FirstName" size = "20">
<input type = "text" name = "LastName" size =
     "20"></td> </tr>
<tr> <td width= "39%" align = "right" ><b>
Email:</b></td> >td width = "61%"><input type =
     "text" name="Email" size = "40">
</td></tr> </table>
```

Each field in this section is created with an INPUT element and has a name and size.

```
<b>How did you find us?</b> <select
     name="HowFound">
     <option value = "SearchEngine">Search Engine
     </option>
     <option value = "Newspaper">Newspaper
     </option>
     <option value = "Other">Other </option>
     </select>
<br>
<input type="submit" value="Submit" name="B1" >
<br> <input type="reset" value="Reset" name =
     "B2">
</body></html>
```

In the final section, there are a drop-down menu created with a SELECT element and the *submit* and *reset* buttons created with INPUT elements. The resulting form is shown in Figure 7-1.

There is also a BUTTON element that can display images on its surface, or highly styled text of various colors, font faces, and sizes.

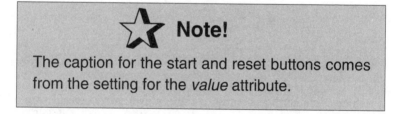

Figure 7-1 The registration form

⭐ Note!

The caption for the start and reset buttons comes from the setting for the *value* attribute.

Drop-down Menus and the SELECT and OPTION Elements

In the registration form example earlier in this chapter, one of the last controls was a drop-down box or menu list created with the SELECT element. This control allows users to quickly view and find one or several choices from among many. Individual OPTION elements make up each option in the list and carry the content and values of each option. Starting and ending tags are required for the SELECT element.

The SELECT element has a *size* attribute that determines the number of rows of options displayed in the drop-down box. Including the *multiple* attribute causes the element to allow more than one choice to be selected. Within the SELECT element each choice in the list is created by an OPTION element. A valid SELECT element must contain at least one OPTION element. Authors can specify the *selected* attribute for an option, in which case that option is preselected when the form is loaded.

The TEXTAREA Element

The TEXTAREA element allows the author to specify a control capable of holding many lines of text. Often this control is used as a comments field. Starting and ending tags are required for the TEXTAREA element, and the core attributes and intrinsic events are supported.

The *name* attribute assigns a name to the control, and the *rows* and *cols* attributes specify the number of rows and number of columns into which the user may enter text, columns being equivalent to characters. For example, a TEXTAREA element assigned 4 rows of 50 columns will produce a box on screen that has space for 4 rows of text with 50 characters in each row. Naturally, how this is rendered depends upon the default font for the browser. There is no attribute limiting the amount of text a user may enter. The following code would produce a text box with 10 rows and 20 characters across:

```
<textarea rows = "10" cols = "20"> </textarea>
```

Using Server-Side and Client-Side Scripting

HTML, although it serves its intended purposes fairly well for now, is not considered a programming language because it does not allow for processing information, only the display of information. It is primarily for the formatting and display of text, images, multimedia, hypertext links, and

HTML forms, with tables and frames thrown in to provide added display capability.

In order to process information, either within the client's browser or back at the server, some programming language must be employed. To maintain broad platform capability, the language must run on most browsers. The language of choice is currently JavaScript, an interpreted language with limited ability to perform standard programming language functions. JavaScript has these limitations so that the possibility of contracting a virus as a result of loading a Web page are minimized.

JavaScript commands are inserted directly into the HTML and are interpreted as the browser reads through the code, rather than being compiled as executable binary files. This means the source code is readily available to users (simply by clicking View|Source from the browser menu), and it also means the code runs slower than compiled programs, in most cases. However, because JavaScript programs tend to be much smaller and more narrowly focused than ordinary compiled applications, humans do not usually notice the speed difference.

JavaScript can perform functions, referred to as *client-side scripts*, that ordinary HTML cannot. JavaScript may also be used to run programs on the server, and these are referred to as *server-side scripts*. On the server, since the platform is known in advance, many scripting languages, programming languages, and application-development technologies may be used. For example, VBScript and PERL are common as back-end languages, as well as Visual Basic and Visual C++. New languages and technologies are being introduced rapidly, and the programming language landscape is in constant flux.

Microsoft's ASP is a technology highly favored in programming circles for the ease it brings to dealing with Website programming and database applications. Notice that ASP is called a technology, rather than a programming language. The reason for this designation is that ASP consists of a set of built-in objects and a processing engine, and these objects may be processed using any scripting language for which an engine is installed on the server.

Note!

Client-side scripts are incorporated into the HTML as part of the page and processed within the client or from the browser. Server-side scripts are processed on the server and may be standalone applications or incorporated into HTML as well.

Using Client-Side Scripting with the DOM

The Document Object Model (DOM) for HTML allows all objects (windows, pages, forms, controls, text blocks, and so on) to be addressed and referred to by *name* or *id* in a hierarchy of objects. A FORM element is a child of a document, and a control is a child of a FORM element, and so on. Objects can be referenced by a script by their *name*, *id*, or within an indexed list based on the hierarchy of objects occurring in a page. For example, the window object is the highest level object and is always present, and referencing a form control (named formcontrol) may be done like this:

```
MyVar = window.document.form.formcontrol
```

Once a reference to an object is established, the events affecting it may be detected and used to trigger processing. The properties of an object may also be read and in some cases changed, such as changing the background color of the BODY element from white to black. Finally, methods may be invoked, performing specific processing functions.

Events occur during a session with a Web page, such as the loading of the page, the loading of the BODY element, the placing of a mouse over an image, the changing of some text in a control, and so forth. When events occur, scripts can be activated. Scripts written within the SCRIPT element are executed when the document is loaded, while scripts that are part of an element run when events supported by that element occur.

The SCRIPT Element

The SCRIPT element inserts a script within a document, and there may be multiple scripts within the HEAD and BODY elements of an HTML page. Although JavaScript seems to be the language of choice, HTML itself does not specify a preference for one language over another. The browser loading a page must recognize and be capable of utilizing the scripting language specified.

Both the starting and ending tags are required for the SCRIPT element, and the *src* attribute may specify an external file (via URL) containing the contents of the script. The *type* attribute specifies the scripting language for the script, as does the deprecated *language* attribute, the difference being that the *type* attribute specifies the language as a content type (text/JavaScript) while the *language* attribute uses a string (JavaScript). The *type* attribute must be specified.

The *defer* attribute, when included, takes no value but tells the browser the script returns no content, so the browser can continue rendering the page without interruption. The *charset* attribute specifies the character encoding of the script designated by the *src* attribute, but not the content of the SCRIPT element. When browsers do not recognize the SCRIPT element they may be inclined to print the contents of the SCRIPT element as plain text. Therefore, scripting language developers have made provisions in their processing engines to read scripting commands embedded in HTML comment tags between the starting and ending SCRIPT tags. For example, the following code shows JavaScript commands in a SCRIPT element, within HTML comment tags:

```
<script type="text/javascript">
<!-scripting commands hidden in here
  function pressbutton(){
    alert("Hello")
}
-->
</script>
```

Intrinsic Events

Many of the elements covered so far support intrinsic events, and some support additional events. Associating scripts with events provides a

Table 7-1 Intrinsic events

NAME:	OCCURS WHEN:	USED WITH:
Onload	The browser completes loading a window or all frames of a page.	BODY, FRAMESET
Onunload	The document is removed from the window or frame	BODY, FRAMESET
Onclick	The mouse arrow is over an element and the button is clicked	Most elements
Ondblclick	The mouse arrow is over an element and the button is clicked twice	Most elements
Onmousedown	The mouse arrow is over an element and the button is held down	Most elements
Onmouseup	The mouse arrow is over an element and the button is released	Most elements
Onmouseover	The mouse arrow is over an element	Most elements
Onmousemove	The mouse arrow is over an element an is moved	Most elements
Onmouseout	The mouse arrow is over an element and is moved out of the element	Most elements
Onfocus	The element receives focus	A, AREA, LABEL, INPUT, SELECT, TEXTAREA, BUTTON
Onblur	The element loses focus	Same as *Onfocus*
Onkeypress	A key is pressed and released while over an element	Most elements
Onkeydown	A key is pressed down and held while over an element	Most elements
Onkeyup	A key is released while over an element	Most elements
Onsubmit	A form is submitted	FORM
Onreset	A form is reset	FORM
Onselect	A user selects text in a text control	INPUT, TEXTAREA
Onchange	The value of a control has been changed and then it loses focus	INPUT, SELECT, TEXTAREA

means of controlling program flow based on user interaction with Web pages and their elements. The intrinsic events are given in Table 7-1.

The NOSCRIPT Element

Like the NOFRAMES element, the NOSCRIPT element serves the purpose of shielding non-script supporting browsers from a total lack of content. If the NOSCRIPT element is present, authors can use it to provide content and HTML tags that will display content only if the browser doesn't support scripting, or if the browser doesn't recognize the language specified. Both the starting and ending tags are required, and the core attributes and intrinsic events are supported.

Solved Problems

Solved Problem 7.1

Show the code for placing a JavaScript in the HEAD element of an HTML page. Make the script hidden from browsers that do not understand JavaScript, and make the script create a function, named "sayhi", to put an alert box on screen telling the user "HI".

Solution:

```
<head> <script language="JavaScript">
<!--
function sayhi() {
alert("Hi")
}--> </script></head>
```

Solved Problem 7.2

Show the code for activating the "sayhi" function when a text box loses focus.

Solution:

```
<input type = "text" size = "20"
name="mytextbox" onblur ="sayhi()">
```

Chapter 8
CASCADING STYLE SHEETS AND DYNAMIC HTML

- ✔ *Style in HTML Pages and Style Sheets*
- ✔ *CSS2 Selectors and Syntax*
- ✔ *Creating Style References in Inline Elements*
- ✔ *The STYLE Element*
- ✔ *Conditional Use of Style Properties with Media Types*
- ✔ *Style Sheet Files and External Style Sheets*
- ✔ *Cascading Style Sheets*
- ✔ *Dynamic HTML*
- ✔ *Using Scripts to Dynamically Modify Attributes and Content*
- ✔ *Solved Problems*

93

In many of the chapters so far the HTML elements covered, while still supported in the popular browsers, have been deprecated in favor of style sheets. *Cascading style sheets* refers to a special processing method by which multiple style sheets may be applied to a single Web page but is not supported by all style sheet languages.

Using style sheets to apply stylistic formatting to Web page elements has a number of advantages over the traditional method of using individual element attributes to modify style. For example, style sheets can be separate documents available to many pages in a Website, enabling the author to apply identical styles across many documents, while only having to modify styles in one file. A change to styles in that one file will automatically modify styles in whatever Web pages are linked to it.

Style in HTML Pages and Style Sheets

Style sheets refer to code written in a special syntax/language that can be used to apply stylistic formatting to a single element, an entire document, or multiple documents from separate files. A style sheet command consists of the *selector*, which matches one or more elements, and the *declaration*, which declares the property affected and the value that property should take for the elements selected. The following code gives a simple example of using an external file for retrieving style information:

```
<html><head><title>Style Sheet Demo 1</title>
<link href="externalstyle1.css" rel="stylesheet"
type="text/css">
</head>
<body bgcolor="#FFFFFF">
<p class="parastyle">This paragraph has brown
text.
<p>This paragraph does not.
</body></html>
```

The code in the example above links the current HTML page to the external style sheet file named "externalstyle1.css". Setting the *rel* attribute to "stylesheet" makes this a persistent style sheet, and setting the *type* attribute to "text/css" tells the browser what style sheet language is being used. The contents of the style sheet file, written in plain text, are:

```
p.parastyle {
color : brown;
}
```

In the style sheet file the lowercase p is the selector, and immediately following it (after the dot) is the name of the class this selector is associated with. This name is created by the author of the document and can be applied to any P elements desired (notice that in the HTML file the *class* attribute of the first paragraph is assigned a value of "parastyle").

The color attribute of P elements is set in the external style sheet file to "brown" via the declaration, and this color is then applied to any P elements in the HTML file whose class attribute is set to "parastyle". If a P element has no class attribute value, or a different one, then this external style sheet has no effect. However, if no class is referenced in the external style sheet, the style given to that selector will be applied to all P elements by default.

Because there are many style sheet languages that may be applied to a document, it is important to set the language an author wishes to use. This can be done by inserting the identifier for the language into a META element, as shown here:

```
<meta http-equiv="Content-Style-Type"
content ="text/css2">
```

CSS2 Selectors and Syntax

Selectors are used to identify the elements to which a particular style will apply and in their most basic form are simply the same as element names. For example, the P selector above refers to the P element. However, CSS2 is termed a style sheet language, and because there are many ways authors might want to identify elements, there are many ways CSS2 can target elements.

For example, the asterisk can be used as a *universal* selector, matching all elements in a document. A *type* selector is equivalent to the element name it is intended to match. A *type* selector could be any element followed by the appropriate properties (such as color) and their values (such as brown). But there are also more complex selectors such as *descendant* selectors, which occur within the context of another element (italicized text within an H element, for instance). Generally, the syntax of CSS2 resembles the example already given. The following code makes all H2 elements, not just those of a particular class, appear green and italicized:

```
H2 { color : green; font-style : italic;}
```

Notice that the properties and their values appear within curly braces, properties and values are separated by colons, and property-value pairs end with semi-colons. Each property-value pair is called a *declaration* or *rule*, and they can be on separate lines or on the same line.

Remember

A style sheet selector is a reference to an HTML element. For example, the style sheet selector P refers to the P element in HTML. Styles applied to the P selector may affect P elements in a Web page.

Creating Style References in Inline Elements

One of the core attributes applicable to just about every HTML element is the *style* attribute. This attribute can be set for any appropriate property-value pair, thereby modifying the style of that element alone. For example, the following code changes the style for a single paragraph within an HTML document, without using the STYLE element or external style sheets:

```
<ul>
    <li>Option 1</li>
    <li>Option 2</li>
```

```
<li style="font-weight : bold;">Option 3
Bold</li>
   <li>Option 4</li>
</ul>
```

Notice the selector is not necessary, because the style information appears within the element itself. Also, it only applies to that single LI element and no other. Remember, the syntax for the property-value pair depends on the style sheet language used.

The STYLE Element

The STYLE element should be used inside an HTML document to create style sheet settings in a group. Style sheet settings can be made for all elements, a single element, elements of a class, or individual elements identified with an id attribute. Typically these settings are found in the HEAD element of a document. Multiple STYLE elements can be present in the HEAD element, as well as multiple rules within a single STYLE element, like this:

```
<head>    <style type="text/css2">
<!--
h2 {text-align : center}
p {color : brown}
       -->
</style> </head>
```

Notice that there is no need for the ending semicolon when only one property-value pair is present for a selector. Notice that there are HTML comment delimiters in the style sheet example. HTML comment delimiters are included so older browsers will skip the style sheet commands. Both the starting and ending tags are required for the style element.

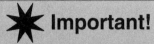 **Important!**

Selectors and settings inside STYLE elements may be interpreted as text by older browsers. Therefore, authors may enclose style settings inside the STYLE element with HTML comment delimiters, like so:

```
<style>
<!--
   p.thepara{color:green; font-size: 10 pt}
-->
</style>
```

The *lang*, *dir*, and *title* attributes are supported by the STYLE element as well as the *type* and *media* attributes. The *type* attribute can be used to specify the content type for the style language (such as "text/css2"), and the *media* attribute can be used to specify the media to which the style applies (the default is "screen", meaning the style will be implemented on a screen).

To set styles for HTML elements of a class, the class name is first applied to the elements using their *class* attributes, like this:

```
<p class="style1">Any paragraph of this class
has this style</p>
```

Next, the STYLE element is added to the HEAD of the document, with the class following the selector using dot notation (a period after the selector and then the class name), thus:

```
<head> <style type="text/css2">
     p.style1 {color : brown}
     </style> </head>
```

Finally, to differentiate *id* from *class* (identifying elements not by selector, but by the *id* attribute), the pound sign is used, as in:

```
<head> <style type="text/css2">
      #astyle {color : brown}
      </style> </head>
<p id="astyle">Any paragraph of this id has this
style>/p>
```

Here is an example using DIV to apply a style to multiple blocks.

```
<html><head><title>New Page 1</title>
<style>
<!-
div.thediv {color: #00FF00; font-size: 18pt;
font-variant: small-caps}
-->
</style>
</head><body>
<div class="thediv">
<p>Paragraphs within the DIV element have text
that is green, 18 points, and small caps</p>
</div>
</body></html>
```

Conditional Use of Style Properties with Media Types

The *media* attribute of the STYLE element allows authors to choose style settings based on the media in which the content will be rendered. When a *media* attribute value is specified, the browser only loads style sheet information for the rendering media.

Approved values for the *media* attribute are called *media descriptors*. The list is not yet a recommendation, and so may change, but here are some of them:

- "all" – Can be rendered on all devices.
- "aural" – Can be rendered on speech synthesizers.
- "Braille" – Can be rendered on Braille tactile feedback devices.
- "handheld" – Can be rendered on handheld devices.
- "tv" – Can be rendered on television-type devices.

An example of code setting various media types for the STYLE element is:

```
<head>
    <style type="text/css2" media="tv">
      p {font-size: 24pt}
    </style>
    <style type="text/css2" media="handheld">
      p {font-size: 8pt}
    </style>
</head>
```

Style Sheet Files and External Style Sheets

Style sheets may also be referenced from an external file. Using the LINK element, an external style sheet can be referenced with a URL pointing to the style sheet, written in plain text. The *href* attribute of the LINK element is used for this purpose. The LINK element must be placed in the HEAD element which may contain any number of external style sheets. The *rel* and *title* attributes are used to determine whether the style sheet is persistent, preferred or alternate. The meaning of these is:

- Persistent – Contains formatting that must be applied regardless of whatever other styles are applied. *rel* is set to "stylesheet" and there is no *title* attribute.
- Alternate – Users can choose from among a number of style sheets. *rel* is set to "alternate stylesheet" and the *title* attribute is provided with a name for the alternate style sheet
- Preferred – Browser should use the style sheet chosen by the author unless the user deliberately chooses another. *rel* is set to "stylesheet" and the *title* attribute is provided with a name for the preferred style sheet.

The *media* attribute can be used with the LINK element and has the same result as in the STYLE element.

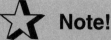

Note!

External style sheet files will only be loaded for the media in use.

Cascading Style Sheets

Some style sheet languages (such as CSS2) have the ability to incorporate elements from several style sheets into one document, according to a set of rules. This ability is called the ability to *cascade*. One set of formatting characteristics is "poured" in, and then another set "cascades" in, and so forth. Technically, the styles are applied for the style sheet encountered first, but succeeding styles are applied preferentially, the last style encountered having the final say.

In the following example, the user is presented with several alternate style sheets to choose from: alt for "first.css" and alt2 for "third.css". If the user chooses "alt", styles from both style sheets (the one named first.css and the one named second.css) are mixed together and applied. The persistent style sheet named basic.css is applied in all cases.

```
<link rel="alternate stylesheet" title="alt"
href="first.css" type="text/css2">
<link rel="alternate stylesheet" title="alt"
href="second.css" type="text/css2">
<link rel="alternate stylesheet" title="alt2"
href="third.css" type="text/css2">
<link rel="stylesheet" href="basic.css"
type="text/css2">
```

Note!

The Cascading Style Sheets Level 2 (CSS2) specification is a current version of one style sheet language, but it is not the only one. It is important because the major browsers support it, even though it is not part of the HTML recommendation.

Dynamic HTML

Dynamic HTML (DHTML) is an odd step-child of ordinary HTML, and in fact it has no formal mention anywhere in the HTML 4.01 recommendation. Instead, the recommendation refers to an author's ability, with scripts, to dynamically reassign the attribute values and content of coded HTML elements. Essentially, DHTML is the name given to this ability, but it means different things within the various browsers.

Within Internet Explorer, the SPAN element is used to apply dynamically changing styles and positioning for a particular element or set of elements, while Netscape extends HTML with the LAYER tag, which performs essentially the same function (except that Navigator 4 and below do not allow dynamic changes to properties). In both cases, the bulk of the documentation refers to how to define a section, define styles, and change them (and content) with scripting languages.

Using Scripts to Dynamically Modify Attributes and Content

As mentioned previously, there are many events supported by HTML elements (as objects), and within scripting languages additional objects may be referenced, including the entire window displaying the contents of a Web page.

When a document is loaded, the page load event may fire, and scripts can detect and use this as a trigger for executing script commands, including the modification of content values (such as text or an image) or attribute values (such as what color the background is or the location on screen of an element).

The HTML recommendation offers a few rules for processing dynamic modifications. In practice these rules mean that the browser reads through the document, processes each SCRIPT element in order, replaces the elements with the results of its processing, and then rebuilds the page accordingly.

Microsoft and Netscape have differing interpretations and implementations of DHTML, but many of the principles used are the same.

Solved Problems

Solved Problem 8.1

Show the code for referencing a persistent external style sheet in a file named "mystyle.css" in which all elements on a page are rendered green. What makes the style sheet persistent?

Solution:

```
<html><head><title> Green Style Sheet
Demo</title>
<link href="mystyle.css" rel="stylesheet"
 type="text/css">
</head>
<body bgcolor="#FFFFFF">
<p>This paragraph has green text.</p>
<p>So does this paragraph.</p>
</body></html>
```

Within the style sheet file the following code, using the wildcard selector *, sets all elements to be rendered green:

```
*{color:green}
```

The style sheet is considered persistent because the *rel* attribute is set to "stylesheet" and there is no *title* attribute.

Solved Problem 8.2

Using a STYLE element, show the HTML and CSS2 code that would be appropriate for making a block of several paragraphs, images, and a form all have a background color of turquoise.

Solution:

For the STYLE element, the code might look like this:

```
<style>
 <!--
div.myblock {background-color: #00FFFF}
 -->
 </style>
```

For the block of paragraphs, images, and the form, the code might look like this:

```
<div class="myblock">
  <p>First paragraph</p>
  <p>Second paragraph</p>
  <img src="myimage.gif">
  <form method="POST"
action="myasppage.asp">
    form contents</form>
  </div>
```

Chapter 9
THE XHTML
SPECIFICATION

What is XHTML 1.0?

XHTML 1.0 is actually the World Wide Web Consortium's (W3C) next iteration of the HTML standard. XHTML itself is a series of document types that conform to the XML standard. XML is discussed in greater detail in Chapter 10.

XHTML is closely related to HTML but is more rigid in its standards for syntax and coding. The purpose of this chapter is to illustrate the differences between HTML and XHTML and offer examples of how to code documents properly with XHTML.

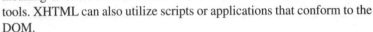

XHTML has some advantages over ordinary HTML. For example, XHTML is XML *conforming*, meaning it can be viewed and edited with XML tools. XHTML can also utilize scripts or applications that conform to the DOM.

XHTML is a logical next step for HTML because of HTML's inherent limitations, and because major browsers seem to respond correctly to XHTML's version of HTML's syntax. HTML cannot be individualized or extended in a very practical way (as is evident from the browser wars in which both the major browser manufacturers introduce their own HTML extensions, which the other rarely supports), while XHTML extensions are relatively easy to support. As an added benefit, if the author follows a few guidelines, XHTML documents can still be understood by older browsers, and so the transition can begin now, rather than waiting for browsers supporting XHTML to appear.

Transitional, Strict, and Frameset XHTML

As for HTML, there are three DTDs for XHTML: *transitional*, *strict*, and *frameset*. The frameset version supports everything in the transitional version plus framesets, while the strict version is useful for highly conforming code that doesn't include deprecated elements and attributes. To specify one of these versions you must include the DTD line at the beginning of your document. See section, "All Documents Must have a DOCTYPE Declaration," for more details.

Converting HTML Documents to XHTML

Web authors are sure to ask what tools are available for converting standard HTML documents to XHTML documents, as it seems likely that the translation can be accomplished by following fairly well-defined procedures, and performing the translation by hand would be tedious and prone to error. The World Wide Web consortium maintains a tool named

"HTML Tidy" at its Website (www.w3.org). HTML Tidy is a free download, and it cleans up regular HTML code. This is the first step in conversion. You can then use the tool to convert HTML code into a format compatible with XHTML. One of the benefits of converting HTML documents to XHTML is they can be processed by XML-capable browsers, a likely requirement in the future, in view of XML's increasing popularity.

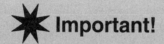 **Important!**

HTML Web pages that work in the popular browsers often have errors that are simply forgiven or overlooked by the browsers. For example, authors sometimes neglect to put attribute values in quotes. This must be corrected before a tool like HTML Tidy can be used to convert the document.

The Modularization of XHTML

The authors of XHTML 1.0 have broken the language into a number of modules that are defined using the XML DTD language and expect to redefine these modules using XML Schemas when this standard is ready. The purpose for modularization is to create separate intact subsets of XHTML functionality, so that the modules may be combined to form a coherent complete language and also so the modules may be used with other, yet-to-be-defined modules created by anyone with an interest in using XHTML as a content language no matter what platform the content is to be rendered on.

Essentially, XHTML modules are language building blocks oriented towards user interface and display, while XML languages (of which XHTML is one) are general purpose languages suitable not only for user interface and display, but for machine interface and communication as well. The beauty of modularized XHTML is that it lends itself to building new user interface and display (or rendering) easily, using modules of the language appropriate for a particular platform. One of the goals of modularization is to help browser makers avoid the "extension" syndrome, whereby each new version of a browser supports some but not all of the core HTML elements and only certain proprietary extensions to HTML.

Abstract Modules

Each XHTML document consists of a set of modules, and abstract modules give meaning to the data. In a given module, the data is semantically different from any other module, and the abstract module helps people understand what that data means by explaining the contents in simple terms rather than only being machine-readable. The modules can then be combined to make coherent documents without the author necessarily understanding every aspect of the underlying structure of the data in the modules.

Building Abstract Modules

Certain conventions are followed when writing XHTML modules, to make them understandable and coherent. For example, if an element is to be included in a module, its name must be listed. If sets of element names are defined (called *content sets*), the names of these sets will be listed. If expressions are allowed, the frequency with which they are allowed can be set with *wildcards*, such as the question mark ? (meaning zero or one instance of an expression is allowed), the asterisk * (zero or more instances allowed), the plus sign + (one or more), and so forth.

XHTML module elements have content types that are allowed, just like HTML. For example, an element may be "EMPTY" (having no content) or "PCDATA" (parsed character data or text) and so forth. XHTML element attributes also have allowable types, such as "CDATA" (character data) "ID" (document-unique identifiers), and so forth. In addition to the ordinary HTML attribute value types, XHTML adds a few new ones, such as "DATETIME", making XHTML more like traditional languages.

Differences Between HTML and XHTML

Making the conversion to XHTML is not very difficult for HTML authors and in many cases simply tightens up coding practices. As mentioned, there are tools available to convert existing HTML pages to XHTML pages, but many authors find it necessary to understand hand-coding XHTML in the same way they understand hand-coding HTML. Hand-coding HTML (and XHTML) is often necessary when writing front-end or back-end scripting code such as JavaScript, Perl, or Active Server Pages, whose output may include plain HMTL or XHTML. Here is a list of the main differences, and the next sections will explain them more carefully.

The primary differences between HTML and XHTML

- All documents must have a DOCTYPE declaration.
- The root element of the document must be <html>.
- Elements and attributes must be lowercase.
- Attribute values must be encased in quotes and not minimized.
- Leading and trailing spaces in attribute values will be stripped.
- Only the *id* attribute can be used to identify an element uniquely.
- Non-empty elements must be terminated or have an ending tag.
- Elements must be nested, not overlapping.
- SCRIPT and STYLE elements must be marked as CDATA areas.

All Documents Must Have a DOCTYPE Declaration

The DOCTYPE declaration for HTML was discussed in Chapter 2, and it is optional for HTML documents. The DOCTYPE declarations for XHTML are based on those for HTML and may change somewhat before being finalized as a recommendation. Essentially, they serve to inform programs what legal syntax is within an XHTML document just as they would for an XML document of any type.

In XHTML all documents are required to have a DOCTYPE declaration and it must occur before the root element in the document, such as (for the Frameset DTD):

```
<!DOCTYPE html PUBLIC "-//W3C//DTD XHTML 1.0
Frameset//EN" "http://www.w3.org/TR/xhtml1/DTD/
frameset.dtd">
```

One of the three DTDs (Strict, Transitional, and Frameset) may be used.

 **Note!**

If an HTML document contains style information within FONT or TABLE tags, the Transitional DTD should be used for the XHTML document it is converted to, otherwise older browsers that don't support style sheets may not render elements as intended.

The Strict DTD is used when style sheets provide for all style information; the Transitional DTD is used when deprecated HTML elements and attributes are used; and the Frameset DTD is used when the document has frames.

The Transitional DTD DOCTYPE declaration is:

```
<!DOCTYPE html PUBLIC "-//W3C//DTD XHTML 1.0
Transitional//EN" "http://www.w3.org/TR/xhtml1/
DTD/transitional.dtd">
```

The Strict DTD DOCTYPE declaration is:

```
<!DOCTYPE html PUBLIC "-//W3C//DTD XHTML 1.0
Strict//EN" "http://www.w3.org/TR/xhtml1/DTD/
strict.dtd">
```

The Root Element of the Document Must Be <html>

Except for the DOCTYPE declaration, no other elements may come be-
fore the starting <html> tag, and no other elements may come after the
ending </html> tag. Therefore XHTML documents must begin with a
DOCTYPE declaration immediately followed by the starting tag for the
HTML element. The starting tag must also contain a reference to the
XML namespace the document uses.

A *namespace* is a closed set of names that identify tags from a particular DTD. Because XHTML and XML are modularized, there is the
possibility that two different DTDs (for two different modules) will have
tags with the same names but different meanings according to their own
DTD definition. XML namespaces are discussed in greater detail in
Chapter 10, in the section, "XML Namespaces."

Here is an example of the coding for the HTML element in XHTML:

```
<html xmlns="http://www.w3.org/1999/xhtml">
```

Elements and Attributes Must Be Lower Case

Unlike HTML, *XML is case sensitive*, so all elements and attributes are
written lowercase. The value of an attribute (e.g. a URL) may of course
use uppercase letters.

Attribute Values Must Be in Quotes and Must Not Be Minimized

All attribute values must be in quotes, and minimized attributes are not
allowed. Browsers currently allow non-quoted attribute values in some
cases, but not others, so as a rule it is easy (and good coding practice) to
use quoted attribute values anyway.

Minimized attribute values are those where simply entering the name
of the attribute causes its function to occur. For example, in HTML, in an
OPTION element within a SELECT element, including the *selected* attribute without a value makes that option selected when the form is rendered. In XHTML, the attribute must include a specific assignment of the
value, in this case "selected", so the element would be coded:

```
<option selected="selected"
value="thevalue">The Value</option>
```

Leading and Trailing Spaces in Attribute Values Will Be Stripped

If an author includes leading or trailing white spaces in an attribute value, they will be stripped out. If there are white spaces within an attribute value, they will be mapped to a single space between words. For western scripts this is an ASCII space character.

Elements Can Only Use the *id* Attribute

Although the *name* attribute was heavily used in HTML to uniquely identify elements, in XHTML only the *id* attribute can be used. The range of values that may be applied to the *id* attribute is very restricted compared to the old *name* attribute. Finally, the *id* attribute value for an element can only be used once within a document and must be unique, unlike the same *name* attribute values that could be used many times in the same document.

Non-Empty Elements Must Be Terminated

Any elements that have both a starting and ending tag must use both in XHTML. For example, whereas in HTML a paragraph could be delimited by only the starting <P> tag (placed at the end of every paragraph, if desired) in XHTML both the starting and ending tags must be in place.

For empty elements, an ending symbol with a space and a slash must be used, as shown here for the line break tag (<br >):

```
<br />
```

The exception is when a non-empty element is used but has no content (so that it appears empty). In this case the author must not use the syntax above, but instead rely on the syntax using both the starting and ending tags, like this (for a paragraph with no content in it):

```
<p></p>
```

Elements Must Be Properly Nested, Not Overlapping

In HTML, if an H element (a heading) of size 2 is to be italicized, the author can write:

```
<h2><i>Here is the italicized heading</h2></i>
```

In this example the H element starts before the I element and ends before the I element, overlapping it. This is supported in HTML, but not XHTML. In XHTML these elements would have to be properly nested, as shown here:

```
<h2><i>Here is the italicized heading</i></h2>
```

There is no provision in XML to exclude nesting certain elements within one another (as long as it is properly coded) but there are some that should never be nested. They are:

- The a (hyperlink or anchor) element should not contain other a elements.
- The pre element should not contain the img, object, big, small, sub, or sup elements.
- The button element should not contain the input, select, textarea, label, button, form, fieldset, iframe, or isindex elements.
- The label element should not contain label elements.
- The form element should not contain form elements.

Script and Style Elements Must Be Delimited By CDATA Symbols

Elements such as script and style make use of languages other than HTML (such as CSS2 and JavaScript) to perform specialized functions that sometimes include a bit of HTML here and there. Without some way to tell the browser specifically to exclude that HTML (and not to render other parts of a script or style sheet as plain text) browser rendering may be unpredictable. The method for doing this in HTML often means enclosing script or style sheet code in HTML comment tags: effective but inelegant. In XHTML, the method for excluding script and style sheet code is to mark the code in these elements as a "CDATA" section. In the following example the "CDATA" section delimiters take the place of HTML comment markers:

```
<script language="JavaScript">
<![CDATA[
function clickme( ) {
alert ("Hello")
}
  ]]>
</script>
```

If an author is using external style sheets or references to external scripts, a "CDATA" section does not need to be used (and shouldn't be).

XHTML and Cascading Style Sheets

Like HTML, XHTML can make use of style sheets for presentational requirements and, as a matter of fact, this method is specifically recommended. There are a few guidelines for correct presentation of XHTML documents with CSS2. For example, when using CSS2, lowercase element and attribute names should be used, and within a table the tbody element should be explicitly written. It is not implied in XML as it is in HTML.

Solved Problems

Solved Problem 9.1
Convert the following code to XHTML, using the transitional DTD.

```
<HTML><HEAD><TITLE>Registration Form</TITLE>
<META HTTP-EQUIV="Content-Type"
CONTENT="text/html; CHARSET=iso-8859-1">
</HEAD>
<BODY BGCOLOR="#FFFFFF" LINK="#663333">
<FORM METHOD="POST" ACTION="register.asp">
```

Solution:
In this code there is no DOCTYPE declaration, no *xmlns* attribute in the html element, and the attributes and elements are in uppercase.

```
<!DOCTYPE html PUBLIC "-//W3C//DTD XHTML 1.0
Transitional//EN"
"http://www.w3.org/TR/xhtml1/DTD/
transitional.dtd">
<html xmlns="http://www.w3.org/1999/xhtml">
<head>
  <title>Registration Form</title>
  <meta http-equiv="Content-Type"
    content="text/html; charset=iso-8859-1">
</head>
<body bgcolor="#FFFFFF" link="#663333">
<form method="POST" action="register.asp"
name="">
```

Solved Problem 9.2
Identify what must be changed in the following HTML code to convert it to XHTML.

```
<div align="left"><font face="Arial,
Helvetica, sans-serif" color="#663333"
size="-1"><b><font face="Arial, Helvetica,
sans-serif" size="+1" color="#FFFFFF"><font
color="#663333">CHOOSE USER NAME/ PASSWORD
</font></font> </b></font></div></td></tr>
<tr><td width="24%" align="right"><font
face="Arial, Helvetica, sans-serif"
color="#663333" size="-1"><b>User
Name<br><br>Password:</b></font></td>
<td width="76%"><input type="text"
name="UserName" size="20" tabindex="15">
<br><input type="text" name="Password"
size="20" tabindex="16"></td></tr>
<tr bordercolor="#CC9966"
bgcolor="#FFCC99"><td width="24%"
align="right" bgcolor="#CCCCFF"
valign="bottom" height="22"><font
face="Arial, Helvetica, sans-serif"
color="#663333" size="-1"><b>I Saw You In
</b></font></td>
```

Solution:

In this code several input elements use the *name* attribute instead of the *id* attribute, are not terminated properly, and an empty element (the line break) is not properly terminated. Here is the corrected version.

```
<div align="left"><font face="Arial,
Helvetica, sans-serif" color="#663333"
size="-1"><b><font face="Arial, Helvetica,
sans-serif" size="+1" color="#FFFFFF"><font
color="#663333">CHOOSE USER NAME/ PASSWORD
</font></font> </b></font></div></td></tr>
<tr><td width="24%" align="right"><font
face="Arial, Helvetica, sans-serif"
color="#663333" size="-1"><b>User Name
<br />Password:</b></font></td>
<td width="76%"><input type="text"
id="UserName" size="20" tabindex="15">
</input><br /><input type="text"
id="Password" size="20" tabindex="16">
</input></td></tr>
<tr bordercolor="#CC9966"
bgcolor="#FFCC99"><td width="24%"
align="right" bgcolor="#CCCCFF"
valign="bottom" height="22"><font
face="Arial, Helvetica, sans-serif"
color="#663333" size="-1"><b>I Saw You In
</b></font></td>
```

Chapter 10

INTRODUCTION TO XML 1.0 AND THE FUTURE

IN THIS CHAPTER:

- ✔ What is eXtensible Markup Language (XML)?
- ✔ The XML Document Structure
- ✔ Writing XML DTDs
- ✔ XML Schemas
- ✔ XML Namespaces
- ✔ XML Elements and Attributes — Logical Structure
- ✔ XML Processors
- ✔ XML Transformations
- ✔ XML Links (XLink)
- ✔ XML Query

What is eXtensible Markup Language (XML)?

Since XML is not a markup language per se, the question "what is XML?" is not necessarily easy to answer. Perhaps the best concise explanation is that it is a means of creating markup languages conforming to a common standard.

Originally, XML was developed by the World Wide Web consortium (the version we refer to here is XML 1.0) and was designed so that it would fulfill the following goals: be usable on the Internet; provide support for many applications; be compatible with SGML; be easy to use; have no optional features; be human-readable; and be concise.

Because XML can be used so easily to make data available in a consistent way not just to people but to applications (think servers) many industry groups are now in the process of developing their own XML applications suitable for the special terms and definitions that are used within their industries.

An XML processor reads XML documents, and typically provides the results to an application. Microsoft's Internet Explorer 5.0 supports XML 1.0 processing, as well as Namespaces, the DOM, and includes an engine for processing eXentsible Style Sheets (XSL, an XML version of CSS).

The XML Document Structure

An XML document consists of elements, attributes, etc., much like an HTML document, although XML documents can contain declarations, processing instructions, and so forth, more like a traditional executable application.

An XML document may have three parts: a *prolog*, a *body*, and an *epilog*. The prolog and epilog are optional. The prolog may contain comments, version information, processing instructions, and a reference to a specific XML DTD, while the epilog may contain comments and processing instructions. The body consists of one or more elements (defined by the DTD), forming a hierarchical tree structure, and possibly containing character data. In the body, elements are very similar in structure, appearance, and function to HTML pages, except that the elements are quite varied and their meaning may be arbitrarily assigned by the author of the DTD. This is the extensible nature of XML.

The following example shows how some elements may be constructed and arranged in the body of an XML document:

```
<nail_products>
  <nail_polish brand="Contours">
    <color>Light Red</color>
    <price>7.95</price>
    <polish_name>Sizzling Red</polish_name>
  </nail_polish>
</nail_products>
```

Notice the hierarchical structure. For example, within the overall category "nail products," there is the possibility of many such products, only one of which is named here, nail polish. And within the category of nail polish, obviously there may be many formulations and several brands.

In XML, elements may contain other elements, character data, character references, entity references, processing instructions, comments, and CDATA (character data) sections. Elements are defined with angle brackets (< >) and both the starting and ending tags are required, unless the element is an empty element. A starting tag might be <nail_products>, and ending tag might be </nail_products>, and an empty-element tag might be <nail_products></nail_products> or <nail_products/> (with the slash marking the end inside the same tag).

Writing XML DTDs

The main focus of XML is the creation of languages (applications) that support unique and interesting elements and attributes, and this can be done by creating DTDs that conform to XML standards. Another method to define rules for XML documents is to create an XML schema, which will be discussed is greater detail in the section "XML Schemas."

Well-formedness is a concept often used in relation to XML documents, and it means that the document contains only one root element and all other elements in the document are contained inside the root element. Furthermore, none of the document's elements overlap. Where an element is nested inside another element, the nested element is called the *child element*, and the element in which the other is nested is called the *parent element*. Just being well-formed is not enough, though. An XML document is considered *valid* if it has a DTD or schema and if it complies with the rules (constraints) expressed in the DTD. The DTD must appear before the first element in the document.

XML DTD Components

An XML DTD consists of a number of valid components which, using the correct syntax, forms the DTD. Table 10-1 contains the allowable components of an XML DTD, along with a short description of each.

Note that DTDs may contain sections that do not necessarily appear in every version of an XML document. These sections are called *conditional sections*. The following code is a portion of an XML DTD:

```
<!DOCTYPE book [
    <!ELEMENT book (chapter*)>
```

Table 10-1 Allowable components of an XML document

Component	Description
Characters	A character is a single unit of text. Legal characters are tab, carriage return, line feed, and the legal characters of Unicode and ISO/IEC 10646.
White Space	One or more space characters, carriage returns, line feeds, or tabs.
Name (Nmtoken)	A token beginning with a letter or one of several punctuation characters, continuing on with letters, digits, hyphens, underscores, colons, or full stops.
Literals	Any quoted string not containing the quotation mark used as a delimiter for that string.
Markup	Start-tags, end-tags, empty-element tags, entity references, character references, comments, CDATA section delimiters, document type declarations, processing instructions, XML declarations, text declarations, and any white space that is outside the document element and not inside other markup.
Comments	A comment syntax identical to HTML comments, `<!- the comment ->`.
Processing Instructions	Processing commands that pass through to an application.
CDATA Sections	Used to delimit style and script sections, and other areas where the data is not part of the markup.
Prolog and Document Type Declarations	Declarations that the document is an XML document, and what DTDs it uses.

```
<!ELEMENT chapter
(chapter.title,chapter.content)>
<!ELEMENT chapter.title (#PCDATA)>
<!ELEMENT chapter.content (#PCDATA
| example | figure | code )*>
<!ELEMENT example
     ((#PCDATA | code)*)>
<!ELEMENT figure
     ((#PCDATA | language)*)>
<!ELEMENT code
     ((#PCDATA | language)*)>
<!ELEMENT language (#PCDATA)>
]>
```

This code sets the DOCTYPE as a book, and then lists the elements available in the book: chapters, chapter titles, figures, code examples, and so forth.

 **Note!**

Some of the elements appear twice, and it is apparent which elements are child elements of others.

XML Schemas

Another method, more recently developed and rapidly gaining ground, for creating a set of rules by which to validate well-formed XML documents is called XML schemas. In fact, there are two XML schema-related documents under development at the W3C: *XML Schema Part 1: Structures* and *XML Schema Part 2: Data Types*.

Schema is a term well known in database circles, because a database schema identifies relationships between tables, what fields are in a table, what data type fields may assume, and what value ranges are permissible in those fields. An XML schema performs essentially the same function, and also provides for constraints to the sequence in which elements may appear, whether or not elements are empty, and what default values attributes have (as a DTD can).

An XML document that conforms to an XML Schema is called an *instance document*, and it may or may not have a direct reference to the schema to which it conforms. In many cases there will be a reference in the instance document, but sometimes the application processing the document will "already know" where to find the appropriate schema.

Instance documents are normal XML documents. Instead of a DTD dictating their structure, the schema sets the rules. XML schemas lay out the allowable elements and their attributes and also dictate element data types, as can be done for fields in a table in a database. Simple data types resemble ordinary database or programming language data types, such as text, integers, dates, and so forth, while complex data types are assembled from one or more simple data types. For example, a complex data type may contain a component that is text, two components that are numbers, and a date, all in one.

XML schemas also allow the sequence in which elements are found to be set, as well as the number of occurrences, minimum and maximum values, and so on, just like constraints in a database. The following code shows an element in an instance document, and the next example shows the schema to which it conforms:

```
<?xml version="1.0"?>
<nail_polish releaseDate="2000-9-19">
   <marketingManager division="Marketing">
      <name>Dani Johnson</name>
      <title>VP US Marketing</title>
      <phone>858-785-1212</phone>
   </marketingManager>
</nail_polish>
```

This code refers to an element of type nail_polish, having an attribute called releaseDate. The releaseDate attribute is set to data type "xsd:date" in the schema. The element nail_polish has a subelement named marketingManager, which is a complex data type consisting of the name, title, and phone number of the marketing manager for this particular product. The complex type is defined in the schema. The namespace for the schema is set in the first line of the schema, and all elements in the schema use the prefix "xsd" to associate themselves with this namespace.

```
<xsd:schema xmlns:xsd=
  "http://www.w3.org/2000/08/XMLSchema">
  <xsd:element name ="nail_polish"
    type="nail_polishType"/>
  <xsd:attribute name="releaseDate"
    type="xsd:date"/>
  <xsd:complexType
    name="marketingManager">
  <xsd:sequence><xsd:element name="name"
    type="xsd:string"/>
  <xsd:element name="title"
    type="xsd:string"/>
  <xsd:element name="phone"
    type="xsd:string"/>
  </xsd:sequence></xsd:complexType>
</xsd:schema>
```

XML Namespaces

Anyone can create an XML application (language), and XML documents can be composed of a mixture of elements from multiple languages. This is the fundamental capability that makes XML so powerful, but it also leads directly to a problem: how to ensure that elements from different XML languages, which happen to have the same names, are not confused when processed. A *namespace* is the set of names used for elements and so forth.

To make each namespace truly unique (even when the names for two different namespaces may be identical) a URL must be supplied to point to the namespace applied to a particular element. The following code shows an example of a namespace declaration, and why it is unique:

```
<nail_polish
xlmns:nail='http://beauty.org/schema'>
</nail_polish>
```

In this code, the nail_polish element is defined in the schema located at http://beauty.org/schema. Multiple namespaces can be used with a single XML document, as shown in the following code:

```
<?xml version="1.0"?>
<nail_products
xmlns:developmentdate="http://beauty.org/date"
xmlns:releasedate=
     "http://beautycompany.com/date">
<nail_polish name="Hot Pink">
<developmentdate:date>Jan 1, 2000</date>
<releasedate:date>Mar 1, 2000</date>
</nail_polish>
</nail_products>
```

Finally, a single element can also have multiple namespaces applied within it, to use for child elements from a number of namespaces, as shown in the following code:

```
<?xml version="1.0"?>
<nail:nail_polish
xmlns:nail='urn:beauty.products:nails'
xmlns:sku='urn:sku.numbers'>
     <nail:brand>Hot Pink</nail:brand>
     <sku:code>1568491379</sku:code>
</nail:nail_polish>
```

You Need to Know ✔

Because the colon is used to separate parts of an XML namespace declaration, authors should not use the colon in XML element names.

XML Elements and Attributes—Logical Structure

In XML, all elements have names, and the term for element names is Generic Identifier (GI). Elements may (but are not required to) have one or more attributes, and each attribute has a name and a value.

The order of attributes in a tag is not significant, and no attribute may appear in a tag twice. Possible attribute values may be arbitrarily restricted, and the values given must conform to the possible value types listed in the DTD. Also, no less than (<) signs may appear in attribute values. Element and attributes names may not include some reserved characters (X, x, M, m, L, l). Element names in starting and ending tags must match for any given element.

When converting Word documents to HTML documents, Microsoft Word 2002 now converts the Word document into an XML document that can be read using Internet Explorer.

Remember

All XML elements and attributes are written lowercase since XML is case sensitive.

XML Processors

At this point, it should be clear that XML documents are made up of DTDs, schemas, and the markup and content files. The rendered document is created by processing the markup and content against the DTDs and schemas, followed by a transformation for the platform on which the finished document is to be displayed.

To process XML documents an XML processor is required. A number of XML processors are available, including the Microsoft XML processor and the Simple API for XML (SAX). XML processors perform functions akin to browsers (albeit with a great deal more precision and flexibility), and Microsoft's XML processor is shipped with Internet Explorer. As already mentioned, Microsoft Word 2002, when saving Word documents as HTML, actually saves them in XML format, which can then be interpreted by Internet Explorer. Note that often XML processors work in the background for an application such as Internet Explorer or Microsoft Word, and can perform their functions for any application (such as a Web server or a database), not just one in which the final output is human-readable.

You Need to Know

Well-formedness means an XML document contains only one root element, and none of its elements overlap.

XML processors fit into two categories: validating and non-validating. *Validating* processors detect any well-formedness errors, and deviations from the rules and constraints built into the DTD or schema for an XML document. *Non-validating* processors check only for well-formedness.

XML Transformations

XML documents displayed in a browser come out looking as though they were written in HTML. The crucial difference is that XML documents must be transformed before they are displayed in a browser. In fact, much of the power of XML derives from the fact that XML documents can be transformed from XML into whatever other format is required, making XML the ideal standard from which to provide data to humans and machines. So, a single XML document may be transformed to HTML for display in a browser, to a compressed or clipped version of HTML for display on a cell phone or in a PDA, or to some database format or proprietary format for use by a machine-driven application where there is no human interaction at all.

Note!

The same XML document may end up looking quite different depending upon the platform for which it is transformed. In practice it is possible to write a single XML document that can be displayed on any number of platforms.

The W3C has developed what's called *extensible Stylesheet Language* (XSL) to provide a standard way of performing transformations. The most recent version is XSL 1.0, currently a candidate recommendation from the W3C.

As with XML, XSL requires a processor to perform transformations. The processor takes an XML document and its accompanying XSL style sheet and builds the finished product from them. The finished product, of course, is the Web page, PDA display, speech, paginated document, and so forth that the style sheet maker desired. Because the server providing the document can detect the platform on which the XML document is to be displayed or rendered, it is relatively easy to ensure that any given platform receives the appropriate XML document and an XSL style sheet.

XML Links (XLink)

The authors of XML considered it a good idea to provide more power for creating a variety of linking structures in XML documents. There are several candidate recommendations undergoing the review process at the W3C: Xlink, XML Base, and XPointer. We will only look at the first of these.

XML Linking Language (XLink) allows elements that create and describe links between resources to be inserted into XML documents. Resources are defined in this recommendation as "any addressable unit of information or service." Links created with Xlink are explicitly defined as Xlink elements, and six types are included in the recommendation: simple, extended, locator, arc, resource, and title. Two of these (simple and extended) are considered linking elements, while the rest just offer information describing the characteristics of the link.

XLinks can build links between whole resources or just parts of them, and they can link to other XML documents or any other resource. When a link is created between resources, the resources *participate* in the link. The resource at the beginning of a link is called the *starting resource*, the resource at the end is called the *ending resource*, and the act of following the link from beginning to end is called *traversal*. The information required to follow a link (starting and ending resource URLs and the direction in which the link proceeds) is called the *arc*. If the links on either end point to each other, so that clicking on the starting link takes you to the ending link, and upon arrival the ending link becomes a starting link pointing back to the original starting link (which now becomes the ending link) the link is said to be multidirectional.

To write a link conforming to XLink, the XLink namespace must be declared, like this:

```
<somexmlelement
xmlns:xlink="http://www.w3.org/1999/xlink">
</somexmlelement>
```

XLink's namespace provides for attributes that are global and serve to identify an element as a link. They are: *type*, *href*, *role*, *arcrole*, *title*, *show*, *actuate*, *label*, *from*, and *to*. Authors may use these global attributes, along with a reference to the XLink namespace, to include link data in any XML element from any namespace. Non-XLink attributes may also be used, creating a very rich link-producing capability.

Simple XLink links (type = simple) are very similar in structure and capability to standard HTML links (the A element and the IMG element). All they really require is a reference to a resource. Extended XLink links, on the other hand, can be associated with any number of resources, including special links inside themselves, and offer a much richer set of linking and information display possibilities. For example, if an author wants to include within a link a pop-up menu offering a choice of destinations (resources) to click on, XLink extended links can do it.

XML Query

XML Schema gives XML documents a database-like structure, and like Structured Query Language (SQL) for ordinary databases, XML Query provides a query language capable of extracting data from XML documents, and creating new documents based on what has been extracted.

Appendix
HTML
Start Tag
Reference

The following table lists HTML tags, showing the start tags, the function they perform, and how they relate to the major browsers and the World Wide Web Consortium's specifications for HTML.

Start Tag	Function	Netscape Navigator	Internet Explorer	WWW Consortium
<!->	Starts a comment	3.0	3.0	3.2
<!doctype>	Starts the document type			3.2
<a>	Starts an anchor	3.0	3.0	3.2
<abbr>	Starts an abbreviation			4.0
<acronym>	Starts an acronym		4.0	4.0
<address>	Starts an address element	4.0	4.0	4.0
<applet>	Deprecated. Use < object >			
<area>	Starts an area inside an image map	3.0	3.0	3.2
<b>	Starts bold text	3.0	3.0	3.2
<base>	Starts a default reference to external resources	3.0	3.0	3.2
<basefont>	Deprecated. Use < style >			
<bdo>	Starts the direction of text display		5.0	4.0
<big>	Starts big text	3.0	3.0	3.2
<blockquote>	Starts a long quotation	3.0	3.0	3.2
<body>	Starts the body element	3.0	3.0	3.2
 	Inserts a single line break	3.0	3.0	3.2
<button>	Starts a push button		4.0	4.0
<caption>	Starts a table caption	3.0	3.0	3.2

129

Start Tag	Function	Netscape Navigator	Internet Explorer	WWW Consortium
< center >	Deprecated. Use < style >			
< cite >	Starts a citation	3.0	3.0	3.2
< code >	Starts computer code text	3.0	3.0	3.2
< col >	Starts attributes for table columns		3.0	4.0
< colgroup >	Starts groups of table columns		3.0	4.0
< dd >	Starts a definition description	3.0	3.0	3.2
< del >	Starts deleted text		4.0	4.0
< dfn >	Starts a definition term		3.0	3.2
< div >	Starts a section in a document	3.0	3.0	3.2
< dl >	Starts a definition list	3.0	3.0	3.2
< dt >	Starts a definition term	3.0	3.0	3.2
< em >	Starts emphasized text	3.0	3.0	3.2
< fieldset >	Starts a fieldset		4.0	4.0
< font >	Deprecated. Use < style >			
< form >	Starts a form	3.0	3.0	3.2
< frame >	Starts a subwindow (a frame)	3.0	3.0	4.0
< frameset >	Starts a set of frames	3.0	3.0	4.0
< h1 > to < h6 >	Starts header 1 to header 6	3.0	3.0	3.2
< head >	Starts information about the document	3.0	3.0	3.2
< hr >	Inserts a horizontal rule	3.0	3.0	3.2
< html >	Starts an html document	3.0	3.0	3.2
< i >	Starts italic text	3.0	3.0	3.2
< iframe >	Starts an inline subwindow (frame)		3.0	4.0
< img >	Starts an image	3.0	3.0	3.2
< input >	Starts an input field	3.0	3.0	3.2
< ins >	Starts inserted text		4.0	4.0
< kbd >	Starts keyboard text	3.0	3.0	3.2
< label >	Starts a label		4.0	4.0
< legend >	Starts a title in a fieldset		4.0	4.0
< li >	Starts a list item	3.0	3.0	3.2
< link >	Starts a resource reference	4.0	3.0	3.2
< map >	Starts an image map	3.0	3.0	3.2
< menu >	Deprecated. Use < ul >			
< meta >	Inserts meta information	3.0	3.0	3.2
< noframes >	Starts a noframe section	3.0	3.0	4.0
< noscript >	Starts a noscript section	3.0	3.0	4.0
< object >	Starts an embedded object		3.0	4.0
< ol >	Starts an ordered list	3.0	3.0	3.2
< optgroup >	Starts an option group			4.0
< option >	Starts an item in a list box	3.0	3.0	3.2
< p >	Starts a paragraph	3.0	3.0	3.2
< param >	Starts a parameter for an object	3.0	3.0	3.2

Start Tag	Function	Netscape Navigator	Internet Explorer	WWW Consortium
< plaintext >	Deprecated. Use < pre >			
< pre >	Starts preformatted text	3.0	3.0	3.0
< q >	Starts a short quotation		4.0	4.0
< samp >	Starts sample computer code	3.0	3.0	3.2
< script >	Starts a script	3.0	3.0	3.2
< select >	Starts a selectable list	3.0	3.0	3.2
< small >	Starts small text	3.0	3.0	3.2
< span >	Starts a section in a document		3.0	4.0
< strike >	Deprecated. Use < del >			
< strong >	Starts strong text	3.0	3.0	3.2
< style >	Starts a style definition	4.0	3.0	3.2
< sub >	Starts subscripted text	3.0	3.0	3.2
< sup >	Starts superscripted text	3.0	3.0	3.2
< table >	Starts a table	3.0	3.0	3.2
< tbody >	Starts a table body		4.0	4.0
< td >	Starts a table cell	3.0	3.0	3.0
< textarea >	Starts a text area	3.0	3.0	3.2
< tfoot >	Starts a fixed table footer		4.0	4.0
< th >	Starts a table header	3.0	3.0	3.2
< thead >	Starts a fixed table header		4.0	4.0
< title >	Starts the document title	3.0	3.0	3.2
< tr >	Starts a table row	3.0	3.0	3.2
< tt >	Starts teletype text	3.0	3.0	3.2
< u >	Deprecated. Use < style >			
< ul >	Starts an unordered list (bullets)	3.0	3.0	3.2
< var >	Starts a variable	3.0	3.0	3.2

Index